On Ethics and Economics

D1262321

The Royer Lectures

Series Editor: John M. Letiche
University of California, Berkeley

On Ethics and Economics

Amartya Sen

Basil Blackwell

Copyright © Amartya Sen 1987

First published 1987
First published in paperback 1988

Basil Blackwell Ltd
108 Cowley Road, Oxford OX4 1JF, UK

Basil Blackwell Inc.
432 Park Avenue South, Suite 1503
New York, NY 10016, USA

All rights reserved. Except for the quotation of short passages for the purposes of criticism and review, no part of this publication may be reproduced, stored in a retrieval system, or transmitted, in any form or by any means, electronic, mechanical, photocopying, recording or otherwise, without the prior permission of the publisher.

British Library Cataloguing in Publication Data

Sen, Amartya
  On ethics and economics.
  1. Economics—Moral and ethical aspects
  I. Title
  174'.4   HB72

  ISBN 0-631-15494-9
  ISBN 0-631-16401-4 Pbk

Typeset in 11 on 13 pt Times
by Columns of Reading
Printed in Great Britain by
Billing & Sons Ltd, Worcester

To Ken Arrow

Contents

Contents

Foreword

This small book is a 'treasure-chest' for economists, philosophers and political scientists interested in the relations between contemporary economics and moral philosophy. Written in a clear, crisp and stimulating style, Professor Amartya Sen provides more than a terse synthesis of the relevant literature on ethics and economics. In the sense of being substantially new, he shows the contributions that general equilibrium economics can make to the study of moral philosophy; the contributions that moral philosophy and welfare economics can make to mainstream economics; and the harm that the misuse of the assumption of self-interested behaviour has done to the quality of economic analysis.

Sen demonstrates that there has occurred a serious distancing between economics and ethics which has brought about one of the major deficiencies of contemporary economic theory. As he persuasively argues, since the actual behaviour of human beings is affected by ethical considerations, and influencing human conduct is a central aspect of ethics, welfare-economic considerations must be allowed to have some impact on actual behaviour and, accordingly, must be relevant for modern logistic economics. But while logistic economics has had an influence on welfare economics, Sen points out that welfare economics has had virtually no influence on logistic economics.

He shows that both the ethics-related origins and the logistic-based origins of economics have cogency of their own. The logistic approach of modern economics, he emphasizes, has often been extremely productive, providing better understanding of the nature of social interdependence and illuminating practical problems precisely because of extensive use of the logistic approach. The development of formal 'general equilibrium theory' is a case in point, and Sen illustrates its application to critical problems of hunger and famine.

The foundation of Sen's arguments rests, however, in the view that economics, as it has emerged, can be made more productive by paying greater and more explicit attention to the ethical considerations that shape human behaviour and judgment. With illuminating brevity, he analyses certain departures from standard behavioural assumptions of economic theory that may arise from distinct ethical considerations. They may arise from intrinsic evaluations and from instrumental ones, either individually or from the group. Sen draws attention to the various causes from which they may arise, causes that give credence to the instrumental role of contemporary social behaviour. Such behaviour may go against each person's apparently dominant strategy, but group-rationality conditions of a specified type often influence actual behaviour without involving any defect in people's knowledge. In consequence, Sen discusses the ways in which welfare economics can be enriched by paying more attention to ethics; how descriptive economics, prognosis, and policy can be improved by making more room for welfare economics in the determination of individual and group behaviour; and how the study of ethics can, in turn, benefit from a closer contact with economics.

Understandably, though Sen is critical of economics as it stands, he does not think that the problems raised have been adequately dealt with in the ethical literature. Therefore, it is not a problem of merely incorporating the lessons from the ethical literature into economics. Indeed, he suggests that some of the ethical considerations can be helpfully analysed further by using various approaches and procedures now utilized in economics (p. 71). Illustrating this argument by the modern literature on rights and consequences, he notes that if rights are considered not only as primarily legal entities with instrumental use, but rather as having intrinsic value, the literature can be much improved. Furthermore, he sets forth systematic suggestions as to how an adequate formulation of rights and of freedom can make substantial use of consequential reasoning of the type standardly used in general interdependence economics.

In one of his most original discussions, Sen indicates that while the richness of the modern literature of ethics is much greater than has been accommodated in economics, the extremely narrow assumption of self-interested behaviour in economics has impeded the analysis of very significant relationships. Mainstream economic theory, however, identifies rationality of human behaviour with internal consistency of choice and, further, with maximization of self-interest. But, as Sen notes, there is neither evidence for the claim that self-interest maximization provides the best approximation to actual human behaviour nor that it leads necessarily to optimum economic conditions. He refers to free market economies, such as Japan, in which systematic departure from self-interested behaviour in the direction of rule-based behaviour – duty, loyalty and good will – has been extremely important for the achievement of individual and group economic efficiency. An accurate interpretation of Adam Smith, he demonstrates, does not lend support to believers in, and advocates of, a narrow interpretation of self-interested behaviour either in ethics or in economics.

Technically, as Sen demonstrates, under a scheme of extremely limited conditions, welfare economics admits of circumstances in which acting entirely according to self-interest could be ethically justified. But the practical significance of this theorizing is highly questionable. Therefore he identifies the limitations of the 'wellfarist' concepts on which, *inter alia* the analysis is based. By distinguishing between the 'well-being aspect' which covers a person's achievements and opportunities in the context of the individual's personal advantage from the 'agency aspect' which examines them in terms of broader objectives, the analysis goes beyond the pursuit of one's own well being, with productive results. Sen distinguishes between elements of distributive justice and more extensive valuations of the individual or group. This leads to a discussion on 'plurality and evaluation'; 'commensurability'; 'completeness and consistency'; 'impossibility theorems', as well as positive possibility results and constructive characterization. In applying the recent philosophical literature on consequentialism to economics, Sen shows how this reasoning – including interdependence and instrumental accounting – can be combined not only with intrinsic valuation but also with position-relativity and agent-sensitivity of moral assessment. In effect, he shows that under realistic conditions, a broad consequential approach can provide a sensitive as well as robust structure for prescriptive thinking on such fundamental issues as rights and freedom.

Sen demonstrates that departures from standard behavioural assumptions of economic theory – incorporating the most important components of self-centered behaviour – may arise from both intrinsic valuations and instrumental ones, either individually or for the group. This is relevant and applicable to standard economic cases of failure of efficiency, arising from such factors as externalities, non-market interdependences, and lack of credibility in government economic policy. Sen suggests that the incentive problems in tackling such issues may have to be re-formulated if departures from self-interested behaviour are to be admitted into economic analysis. He maintains that what a person, or group, can be seen as maximizing is a relative matter, depending on what appears to be the appropriate control variables and what variations are seen as a right or correct means of control exercised by the agent or group. There may arise a genuine ambiguity when the instrumental value of certain social rules are accepted for the general pursuit of individual goals. Reciprocity in such circumstances must be taken to be instrumentally important, for otherwise it is difficult to argue that one's 'real goals' are to follow reciprocity rather than one's actual goals. By emphasizing that norms and behaviour should become more closely integrated in economic theory, and in providing systematic means of doing so, Sen points the way to further analysis of more specific, alternative welfare criteria.

Members of the Department of Economics and the Department of Philosophy at the University of California at Berkeley are pleased to have had Professor Amartya Sen, an economist and philosopher of truly international distinc-tion, deliver the 1986 Royer Lectures upon which this book is based. We believe the reader will share our gratitude for Professor Sen's timely contribution and our obligation to René Olivieri of Basil Blackwell for expediting publication.

John M. Letiche

Preface

This is an edited version of the Royer Lectures I gave at the University of California at Berkeley during 4–6 April, 1986. I am most grateful to the Departments of Economics, Philosophy and Political Science of that University for their invitation to give these lectures, and for the intellectual stimulation and superb hospitality offered to me when I visited Berkeley.

In preparing the revised text, I have benefited greatly from discussions with Jack Letiche, Martha Nussbaum, Derek Parfit, and Bernard Williams. I have also profited from the comments of Irma Adelman, George Akerlof, Pranab Bardhan, Donald Davidson, John Harsanyi, Jocelyn Kynch, Samuel Sheffler, and Benjamin Ward, and from the engaging discussions following my three lectures. I am also grateful to Emma Dales for excellent copy editing and to Caroline Wise for efficiently typing the manuscript.

Amartya Sen

1 Economic Behaviour and Moral Sentiments

In a not altogether unworthy verse, Edmund Clerihew Bentley had the following to say about a major practitioner of economics – or political economy, as the subject used to be called:

John Stuart Mill
By a mighty effort of will
Overcame his natural bonhomie
And wrote 'Principles of Political Economy'.

While John Stuart Mill should clearly be congratulated for so efficiently subduing his good-natured friendliness, it is not altogether clear what congratulations are due to Political Economy for its alleged demand, to paraphrase Dante, 'Abandon all friendliness, you who enter!' Perhaps the economist might be personally allowed a moderate dose of friendliness, provided in his economic models he keeps the motivations of human beings pure, simple and hard-headed, and not messed up by such things as goodwill or moral sentiments.

While this view of economics is quite widely held (and not without reason, given the way modern economics has evolved), there is nevertheless something quite extraordinary in the fact that economics has in fact evolved in this way, characterizing human motivation in such spectacularly narrow terms. One reason why this is extraordinary is that economics is supposed to be concerned with real people. It is hard to believe that real people could be completely unaffected by the reach of the self-examination induced by the Socratic question, 'How should one live?' – a question that is also, as Bernard Williams (1985) has recently argued, a central motivating one for ethics. Can the people whom economics studies really be so unaffected by this resilient question and stick exclusively to the rudimentary hard-headedness attributed to them by modern economics? Another surprising feature is the contrast between the self-consciously 'non-ethical' character of modern economics and the historical evolution of modern economics largely as an offshoot of ethics. Not only was the so-called 'father of modern economics', Adam Smith, a Professor of Moral Philosophy at the University of Glasgow (admittedly, a rather pragmatic town), but the subject of economics was for a long time seen as something like a branch of ethics. The fact that economics used to be taught at Cambridge until fairly recently simply as a part of 'the Moral Science Tripos' is no more than an instance of the traditional diagnosis of the nature of economics. In fact, in the 1930s when Lionel Robbins in his influential book *An Essay on the Nature and Significance of Economic Science*, argued that 'it does not seem logically possible to associate the two studies [economics and ethics] in any form but mere juxtaposition',[1] he was taking a position that was quite unfashionable then, though extremely fashionable now.

Two Origins

It is, in fact, arguable that economics has had two rather different origins, both related to politics, but related in

---

[1] Robbins (1935, p. 148). Robbins was, of course, well aware that he was contradicting a widely held view.

rather different ways, concerned respectively with 'ethics', on the one hand, and with what may be called 'engineering', on the other. The ethics-related tradition goes back at least to Aristotle. At the very beginning of *The Nicomachean Ethics*, Aristotle relates the subject of economics to human ends, referring to its concern with wealth. He sees politics as 'the master art'. Politics must use 'the rest of the sciences', including economics, and 'since, again, it legislates as to what we are to do and what we are to abstain from, the end of this science must include those of the others, so that this end must be the good for man'. The study of economics, though related immediately to the pursuit of wealth, is at a deeper level linked up with other studies, involving the assessment and enhancement of more basic goals. 'The life of money-making is one undertaken under compulsion, and wealth is evidently not the good we are seeking; for it is merely useful and for the sake of something else.'[2] Economics relates ultimately to the study of ethics and that of politics, and this point of view is further developed in Aristotle's *Politics*.[3]

There is no scope in all this for dissociating the study of economics from that of ethics and political philosophy. In particular, it is worth noting here that in this approach there are two central issues that are particularly foundational for economics. First, there is the problem of human motivation related to the broadly ethical question 'How should one live?' To emphasize this connection is not the same as asserting that people will always act in ways they

---

[2] *The Nicomachean Ethics*, I.1–I.5; in the translation by Ross (1980, pp. 1–7).

[3] While Aristotle discusses the role of the state in economic matters, it is also firmly kept in view that 'the end of the state' is 'the common promotion of a good quality life' (*Politics*, **III**.ix; in the translation by Barker 1958, p. 117). See also *Politics*, **I**. viii–x.

will themselves morally defend, but only to recognize that ethical deliberations cannot be totally inconsequential to actual human behaviour. I shall call this 'the ethics-related view of motivation'.

The second issue concerns the judgement of social achievement. Aristotle related this to the end of achieving 'the good for man', but noted some specially aggregative features in the exercise: 'though it is worthwhile to attain the end merely for one man, it is finer and more godlike to attain it for a nation or for city-states' (*Nicomachean Ethics*, I.2; Ross 1980, p. 2). This 'ethics-related view of social achievement' cannot stop the evaluation short at some arbitrary point like satisfying 'efficiency'. The assessment has to be more fully ethical, and take a broader view of 'the good'. This is a point of some importance again in the context of modern economics, especially modern welfare economics.

The first of the two origins of economics, related to ethics and to an ethical view of politics, does in this way point towards certain irreducible tasks of economics. I shall have to take on presently the question as to how well modern economics has been able to perform these tasks. But before that, I turn to the *other* origin of economics – related to the 'engineering' approach. This approach is characterized by being concerned with primarily logistic issues rather than with ultimate ends and such questions as what may foster 'the good of man' or 'how should one live'. The ends are taken as fairly straightforwardly given, and the object of the exercise is to find the appropriate means to serve them. Human behaviour is typically seen as being based on simple and easily characterizable motives.

This 'engineering' approach to economics has come from several different directions, including – as it happens – being developed by some actual engineers, such as Leon Walras, a nineteenth century French economist who did much to sort out many hard technical problems in economic relations, especially those connected with the functioning of the markets. There were many earlier contributors in this tradition to economics. Even the contributions in the seventeenth century of Sir William Petty, who is justly regarded as a pioneer of numerical economics, clearly had a logistic focus, which was not unrelated to Petty's own interests in the natural and mechanical sciences.

The 'engineering' approach also connects with those studies of economics which developed from the technique-oriented analyses of statecraft. Indeed, in what was almost certainly the first book ever written with anything like the title 'Economics', namely, Kautilya's *Arthaśāstra* (translated from Sanskrit, this would stand for something like 'instructions on material prosperity'), the logistic approach to statecraft, including economic policy, is prominent. Kautilya, who wrote in the fourth century BC, was an advisor and Minister of the Indian emperor Chandragupta, the founder of the Mauryan dynasty (and the grandfather of the more famous Aśoka).[4] The treatise begins in the first chapter with the distinction between 'four fields of knowledge' including (1) metaphysics, and (2) knowledge of 'the right and the wrong', but then it settles down to discussing more practical types of knowledge dealing with (3) 'the science of government', and (4) the 'science of wealth'.

---

[4] There are some disputes about the exact dating of *Arthaśāstra*. The version that is extant seems to have been written some centuries later, and refers to Kautilya in the third person, citing his views, presumably from the earlier version of the document. For English translations see Ramaswamy (1962) and Shama Sastry (1967). See also Krishna Rao (1979) and Sil (1985).

In discussing a great range of practical problems, varying from 'building of villages', 'land classification', 'collection of revenue', 'maintenance of accounts', 'tariff regulations', etc., to 'diplomatic manoeuvres', 'strategy for vulnerable states', 'pact for colonization', 'influencing parties in an enemy state', 'employing spies', 'controlling embezzlement by officers', and so on, the attention is very firmly on 'engineering' problems. The motivations of human beings are specified by and large in fairly simple terms, involving. *inter alia* the same lack of bonhomie which characterizes modern economics. Ethical considerations in any deep sense are not given much role in the analysis of human behaviour. Neither the Socratic question nor the Aristotelian ones figure in this other ancient document of early economics, by a contemporary of Aristotle.

Given the nature of economics, it is not surprising that both the ethics-related origin and the engineering-based origin of economics have some cogency of their own. I would like to argue that the deep questions raised by the ethics-related view of motivation and of social achievement must find an important place in modern economics, but at the same time it is impossible to deny that the engineering approach has much to offer to economics as well. In fact, in the writings of the great economists both the features are noticeable in varying proportions. The ethical questions are obviously taken more seriously by some than by others. For example, it has a greater hold on the writings of, say, Adam Smith, John Stuart Mill (despite what Bentley says), Karl Marx, or Francis Edgeworth, than on the contributions of, say, William Petty, François Quesnay, David Ricardo, Augustine Cournot, or Leon Walras, who were more concerned with the logistic and engineering problems within economics.

Neither kind is, of course, pure in any sense, and it is a question of balance of the two approaches to economics. In fact, many exponents of the ethical approach, from Aristotle to Adam Smith, were deeply concerned with engineering issues as well, within the directional focus of ethical reasoning.

It is arguable that the importance of the ethical approach has rather substantially weakened as modern economics has evolved. The methodology of so-called 'positive economics' has not only shunned normative analysis in economics, it has also had the effect of ignoring a variety of complex ethical considerations which affect actual human behaviour and which, from the point of view of the economists studying such behaviour, are primarily matters of fact rather than of normative judgement. If one examines the balance of emphases in the publications in modern economics, it is hard not to notice the eschewal of deep normative analysis, and the neglect of the influence of ethical considerations in the characterization of actual human behaviour.

Achievements and Weakness

I would argue that the nature of modern economics has been substantially impoverished by the distance that has grown between economics and ethics.[5] I shall try to analyse

---

[5] While the focus of the book is on this problem, it is not, of course, my contention that this is the only major source of difficulties in modern economics. For pointers to various other types of problems, see Kornai (1971, 1985), Ward (1972), Hicks (1979, 1984, 1983), Schelling (1978), Elster (1978, 1979, 1983), Hahn and Hollis (1979), Simon (1979), Blaug (1980), Pitt (1981), Nelson and Winter (1982), Akerlof (1984), Helm (1984, 1985), Matthews (1984), McCloskey (1985). On related methodological issues, see also Robinson (1962), Latsis (1976), Bell and Kristol (1981), Dyke (1981), A.K. Dasgupta (1984), Steedman and Krause (1986), Woo (1986).

the nature of the loss, and the challenge it poses. But in order not to be misunderstood, I would like to make two clarificatory remarks before I proceed further. First, it is not my contention that the 'engineering' approach to economics has not been fruitful. I believe it has often been very fruitful. There are many issues on which economics has been able to provide better understanding and illumination precisely because of extensive use of the engineering approach.

These contributions have been possible *despite* the neglect of the ethical approach, since there are important economic logistic issues that do call for attention, and which can be tackled with efficiency, up to a point, even within the limited format of a narrowly construed non-ethical view of human motivation and behaviour. To give just one illustration, the development of the formal 'general equilibrium theory', dealing with production and exchange involving market relations, have sharply brought out important interrelations that call for technical analysis of a very high order. While these theories are often abstract, not only in the sense of characterizing social institutions in a rather simple form, but also in seeing human beings in very narrow terms, they have undoubtedly made it easier to understand the nature of social inter-dependence. Such interdependence is one of the more complex aspects of economics in general, and the insights derived from these theoretical analyses have proved useful even in practical 'bread and butter' problems.

To illustrate, this is very much the case, for example, in providing a causal analysis of the tragically real problems of hunger and famine in the modern world. The fact that famines can be caused even in situations of high and increasing availability of food can be better understood by bringing in patterns of interdependence which general equilibrium theory has emphasized and focused on. In particular, it turns out that famines often have little to do with food supply, and instead have causal antecedents elsewhere in the economy, related through general economic interdependence (on this see Sen 1981a).

The point here is not only to note that very abstract theoretical models might still be of considerable practical relevance – a fact that must be obvious enough. It is also to emphasize that even the oddly narrow characterization of human motivation, with ethical considerations eschewed, may nevertheless serve a useful purpose in understanding the nature of many social relations of importance in economics. I am, therefore, not arguing that the non-ethical approach to economics must be unproductive. But I would like to argue that economics, as it has emerged, can be made more productive by paying greater and more explicit attention to the ethical considerations that shape human behaviour and judgement. It is not my purpose to write off what has been or is being achieved, but definitely to demand more.

The second clarificatory remark concerns the two-sided nature of the loss as a result of the distance that has grown between economics and ethics. I have so far concentrated on what economics has tended to lose by neglecting the ethics-related views of motivation and social achievement, and indeed I shall explore them further in the rest of this lecture and also in the later ones. But I would also like to argue that there is something in the methods standardly used in economics, related *inter alia* with its 'engineering' aspects, that can be of use to modern ethics as well, and the distance that has grown between economics and ethics has also been, I believe, unfortunate for the latter.

Indeed, while the Aristotelian questions referred to earlier are of obvious importance for economists to think about, it must not be overlooked that the question regarding the role of economics was raised by Aristotle mainly in the context of providing a broad enough view of ethics and politics (*The Nicomachean Ethics*, Book I). Economic issues can be extremely important for ethical questions, including the Socratic query, 'How should one live?'

In fact, quite aside from the direct role of economics in understanding better the nature of some of the ethical questions, there is also the methodological point that some of the insights used in economics in tackling problems of interdependence can be of substantial importance in dealing with complex ethical problems even when economic variables are not involved.

In recent years, a number of moral philosophers have emphasized – rightly in my judgement – the *intrinsic* importance of many considerations that are taken to be of only instrumental value in the dominant ethical school of utilitarian thinking. But even when this intrinsic importance is accepted, the need for instrumental and consequential analysis is not really reduced, since intrinsically important variables may *also* have instrumental roles in influencing other intrinsically important things. As it happens, it is in the pursuit of complex interdependences that economic reasoning, influenced by the 'engineering' approach, has made very substantial strides. In this respect, there is something to be gained for ethics from reasonings of the type much used in economics. There will be an occasion to examine this issue when discussing the nature and importance of consequential analysis in the third lecture.

Economic Behaviour and Rationality

In the rest of this lecture, I shall be concerned primarily with the question of economic behaviour and motivation. The assumption of 'rational behaviour' plays a major part in modern economics. Human beings are assumed to behave rationally, and given this special assumption, characterizing rational behaviour is not, in this approach, ultimately different from describing actual behaviour.

There is quite a substantial issue here, since it can be disputed that it is sensible to approach the problem of predicting actual behaviour by making the concept of rationality act as an 'intermediary'. Even if the characterization of rational behaviour in standard economics were accepted as just right, it might not necessarily make sense to assume that people would *actually* behave in the rational way characterized. There are many obvious difficulties with this route, especially since it is quite clear that we all do make mistakes, we often experiment, we get confused, and so forth. The world certainly has its share of Hamlets, Macbeths, Lears and Othellos. The coolly rational types may fill our textbooks, but the world is richer.

It is, of course, possible to base a critique of modern economics on its identification of actual behaviour with rational behaviour, and such critiques have indeed been forcefully presented.[6] In defence of the assumption that actual behaviour is the same as rational behaviour, it could be said that while this is likely to lead to mistakes, the alternative of assuming any *particular* type of irrationality may very likely lead to even more mistakes. This is a deep question, and I leave it for the moment, though I shall have to return to it later on in this lecture.

Two preliminary points are, however, worth making before we move on. First, it is possible that a view of rationality may admit alternative behaviour patterns, and when that is the case, the assumption of rational behaviour

---

[6] See, in particular, Hirschman (1970, 1982), Kornai (1971), Scitovsky (1976), Simon (1979), Elster (1983), Schelling (1984), Steedman and Krause (1986).

alone would not be adequate in pinning down some 'required' actual behaviour, even with the ultimate objectives and constraints fully specified. Second, the issue of identifying actual behaviour with rational behaviour (no matter how rationality of behaviour is defined) must be distinguished from the issue of the content of rational behaviour as such. The two issues are not unconnected, but they are nevertheless quite distinct from each other. As was mentioned earlier, in standard economic theorizing, these two features have, in fact, often been used in a complementary way. The two together have been utilized to characterize the nature of actual behaviour through the twin process of: (1) identifying actual behaviour with rational behaviour; and (2) specifying the nature of rational behaviour in rather narrow terms.

Rationality as Consistency

How is rational behaviour characterized in standard economic theory? It is fair to say that there are two predominant methods of defining rationality of behaviour in mainline economic theory. One is to see rationality as internal *consistency* of choice, and the other is to identify rationality with *maximization of self-interest*.

Considering the former approach first, the requirement of consistency can be varied, but the standard ones tend to relate – directly or indirectly – to its being possible to explain the set of actual choices as resulting from maximization according to some binary relation. In some formulations only a limited type of binariness is demanded, whereas in others the choice function is taken to be entirely representable by a binary relation – what Richter (1971) calls 'rationalizability'. In even more demanding formulations, the binary relation is required to be fully transitive, and more demandingly still, even representable by a numerical function which the person can be seen as maximizing.[7]

This is not the occasion to go into the analytical differences between the different requirements of internal consistency, or to investigate the extent of congruence that some apparently distinct consistency conditions, in fact, have.[8] However, no matter what these conditions are, it is hard to believe that internal consistency of choice can itself be an adequate condition of rationality. If a person does exactly the opposite of what would help achieving what he or she would want to achieve, and does this with flawless internal consistency (always choosing exactly the opposite of what will enhance the occurence of things he or she wants and values), the person can scarcely be seen as rational, even if that dogged consistency inspires some kind of an astonished admiration on the part of the observer. Rational choice must demand something at least about the correspondence between what one tries to achieve and how one goes about it.[9] It might well be arguable that rational

---

[7] Not all complete orderings are numerically representable (on this, see Debreu 1959).

[8] I have investigated the connections between these relations elsewhere, in Sen (1971, 1977a). See also Hansson (1968), Richter (1971), Herzberger (1973), Fishburn (1974), Kelly (1978), Suzumura (1983), Aizerman (1985), and Schwartz (1986), among others.

[9] Rationality may, of course, be seen as demanding more than this, but scarcely any less. It is possible to argue that what we aim to achieve should also satisfy some criteria of rational assessment (on this see Broome 1978, Parfit 1984, Sen 1985e), so that a purely 'instrumental' concept of rationality may be quite inadequate. But even if such a view is taken, the 'instrumental' role of choice must *inter alia* be accepted. What may be called 'correspondence rationality'

behaviour must *inter alia* demand some consistency, though the issue is far more complex than is often claimed (as I shall argue in the third lecture). But consistency itself can hardly be *adequate* for rational behaviour.

I have tried to argue elsewhere[10] that even the very idea of *purely internal* consistency is not cogent, since what we regard as consistent in a set of observed choices must depend on the *interpretation* of those choices and on some features *external* to choice as such (e.g. the nature of our preferences, aims, values, motivations). Whether or not this rather 'extreme' view, which I believe to be correct, is accepted, it is certainly bizarre to think that internal consistency – no matter how defined – could itself be *sufficient* for guaranteeing a person's rationality.

I should add here that the view of rationality as consistency has been, in some of the literature, made apparently less implausible by the mesmerizing appeal of chosen words. The binary relation underlying choice, when choice has consistency of that type, has sometimes been described as the person's 'utility function'. Needless to say, by construction, such a person can be seen as maximizing that 'utility function'. But this is not adding anything more to what we already knew, and in particular, it is saying really nothing on what it is that the person is trying to maximize. Calling that binary relation the person's 'utility function' does not tell us that it is his or her utility in any

---

– the correspondence of choice with aims, etc. – must be a *necessary* condition of rationality as a whole, whether or not it is also *sufficient*, i.e. whether or not 'correspondence rationality' has to be supplemented by rationality requirements on the nature of the reflection regarding what one should want, value, or aim at (what is called 'reflection rationality' in Sen 1985e).

[10] In my Presidential Address to the Econometric Society in 1984, 'Consistency', to be published in *Econometrica* (Sen 1984c).

independently defined sense (such as happiness or desire-fulfilment) that the person is in fact trying to maximize.

Self-interest and Rational Behaviour

I turn now to the second approach to rationality – that of self-interest maximization. This is, in fact, based on demanding an *external* correspondence between the choices that a person makes and the self-interest of the person. This approach certainly is not open to the criticism made against the internal consistency view of rationality. In terms of historical lineage, the self-interest interpretation of rationality goes back a long way, and it has been one of the central features of mainline economic theorizing for several centuries.

The trouble with this approach to rationality lies elsewhere. Why should it be *uniquely* rational to pursue one's own self-interest to the exclusion of everything else? It may not, of course, be at all absurd to claim that maximization of self-interest is not irrational, at least not necessarily so, but to argue that anything other than maximizing self-interest must be irrational seems altogether extraordinary.

The self-interest view of rationality involves *inter alia* a firm rejection of the 'ethics-related' view of motivation. Trying to do one's best to achieve what one would like to achieve can be a part of rationality, and this can include the promotion of non-self-interested goals which we may value and wish to aim at. To see any departure from self-interest maximization as evidence of irrationality must imply a rejection of the role of ethics in actual decision taking (other than some variant or other of that exotic moral view known as 'ethical egoism'[11]).

---

[11] For a critical examination of different versions of 'ethical egoism', see Williams (1985, pp. 11–15).

The methodological strategy of using the concept of rationality as an 'intermediary' is particularly inappropriate in arriving at the proposition that *actual* behaviour must be self-interest maximizing. Indeed, it may not be quite as absurd to argue that people always *actually* do maximize their self-interest, as it is to argue that *rationality* must invariably demand maximization of self-interest. Universal selfishness as *actuality* may well be false, but universal selfishness as a requirement of *rationality* is patently absurd. The complex procedure of equating self-interest maximization with rationality and then identifying actual behaviour with rational behaviour seems to be thoroughly counterproductive if the ultimate intention is to provide a reasonable case for the assumption of self-interest maximization in the specification of *actual* behaviour in economic theory. To try to use the demands of rationality in going to battle on behalf of the standard behavioural assumption of economic theory (to wit, *actual* self-interest maximization) is like leading a cavalry charge on a lame donkey.

Forgetting rationality for the moment, how good an assumption is self-interest maximization as a characterization of *actual* behaviour? Does the so-called 'economic man', pursuing his own interests, provide the best approximation to the behaviour of human beings, at least in economic matters? That is indeed the standard assumption in economics, and that point of view is not short of supporters.[12] For example, in his Tanner Lectures entitled

---

[12] It has also been disputed from many different points of view, suggesting various alternative structures. See Sen (1966, 1973a, 1974, 1977c), Hirschman (1970, 1977, 1982, 1984, 1985), Nagel (1970), Kornai (1971), Hollis and Nell (1975), Leibenstein (1976), Scitovsky (1976, 1985), Baier (1977), Hirsch (1977), Ullman-Margalit (1977), Broome (1978), Collard (1978), Rose-Ackerman (1978), Schelling

'Economics or Ethics?', George Stigler (1981) has provided a well-articulated defence of the view that 'we live in a world of reasonably well-informed people acting intelligently in pursuit of their self-interests' (p. 190). The evidence for this belief presented by Stigler seems, however, to be largely confined to predictions made by Stigler himself:

> Let me predict the outcome of the systematic and comprehensive testing of behaviour in situations where self-interest and ethical values with wide verbal allegiance are in conflict. Much of the time, most of the time in fact, the self-interest theory (as I interpreted on Smithian lines) will win.[13]

(1978, 1984), Wong (1978), Elster (1979, 1983), Hollis (1979, 1981), Majumdar (1980), Pattanaik (1980), Solow (1980), Winston (1980) Dyke (1981), Putterman (1981, 1986), van der Veen (1981), Akerlof and Dickens (1982), McPherson (1982, 1984), Margolis (1982), Akerlof (1983, 1984), Douglas (1983), Hindess (1983), Frohlick and Oppenheimer (1984), George (1984), Helm (1984a), Parfit (1984), Schick (1984), Davidson (1985a), Diwan and Lutz (1985), Frank (1985), Hirschleifer (1985), Schotter (1985), Steedman and Krause (1986). But it is fair to say despite these (and other) criticisms, the assumption of purely self-interested behaviour remains the standard one in economics, providing the behavioural foundation of standard economic theory and policy analysis, and the basis of much of what is taught to students of economics.

[13] Stigler (1981, p. 176). Later on Stigler argues that 'the utility-maximizing hypothesis is . . . difficult to test, less because of its own ambiguities than because there is no accepted body of ethical beliefs which can be tested for consistency with the hypothesis' (pp. 189-190). One can, however, argue that if indeed there were no ambiguities in the definition of 'the utility maximizing hypothesis', it should be possible to do a testing of the results of that hypothesis *vis-à-vis* *directional* departures towards the interests of others. Also, in testing whether the utility-maximizing hypothesis, if unambiguous, is correct or not, there is no necessity to contrast it with one particular 'accepted body of ethical beliefs'.

Stigler does not reveal his grounds for this prediction excepting his belief that this result 'is the prevalent one found by economists not only within a wide variety of economic phenomena, but in their investigations of marital, child-bearing, criminal, religious, and other social behaviours as well' (p. 176). But the fact is there have been very few empirical testings of this kind, whether in economics, or in such matters as marital relations, or religious behaviour, despite analytically interesting pronouncements by some theorists.[14] While assertions of conviction are plentiful, factual findings are rare. Claims that the self-interest theory 'will win' have typically been based on some special theorizing rather than on empirical verification.

Sometimes the alleged case for assuming self-interested action seems to be based on its expected results – arguing that this would lead to efficient outcomes. The success of some free-market economies, such as Japan, in producing efficiency has also been cited as some evidence in the direction of the self-interest theory. However, the success of a free market does not tell us anything at all about what *motivation* lies behind the action of economic agents in such an economy. Indeed, in the case of Japan, there is strong empirical evidence to suggest that systematic departures from self-interested behaviour in the direction of duty, loyalty and goodwill have played a substantial part in industrial success.[15] What Michio Morishima (1982) calls 'the Japanese ethos' is certainly hard to fit into any simple

---

[14] On this, see Becker (1976, 1981), Posner (1977, 1980), Grossbard (1980), Radnitzsky and Bernholz (1985).

[15] Indeed the hold of rule-based behaviour in Japan can be seen not only in economic matters, but also in other spheres of social conduct, e.g. in the rarity of littering, the infrequency of litigation, an unusually small number of lawyers, and a lower rate of crime, compared with countries of similar affluence.

picture of self-interested behaviour (even taking into account the indirect effects, to which Stigler rightly refers). Indeed, we are beginning to see the development of a whole range of alternative theories about economic behaviour to achieve industrial success, based on comparative studies of different societies with different prevalent value systems (Ronald Dore's 1984 pointer to what he calls 'the Confucian recipe for industrial success' being one interesting example of such alternative theories).[16]

It is worth commenting – at the risk of labouring the obvious – that to deny that people always behave in an exclusively self-interested way is not the same as asserting that they *always* act selflessly. It would be extraordinary if self-interest were not to play quite a major part in a great many decisions, and indeed normal economic transactions would break down if self-interest played no substantial part at all in our choices (on this, see Sen 1983b). The real issue is whether there is a plurality of motivations, or whether self-interest *alone* drives human beings.

A second clarificatory point concerns the fact that the contrast is not necessarily between self-interest, on the one hand, and some kind of a general concern for all, on the other. The traditional dichotomy between 'egoism' and 'utilitarianism' (see Sidgwick 1874, Edgeworth 1881) is misleading in several respects, including the fact that

---

[16] The evolutionary perspective is an important one in this context, on which see Hicks (1969), Hirschleifer (1977, 1985), Guha (1981), Schotter (1981, 1985), Nelson and Winter (1982), Helm (1984a), Matthews (1984). On the biological literature, see Maynard Smith (1982) in addition to Dawkins (1976, 1982) and Wilson (1978, 1980). The simple natural-selection argument for profit maximizing firms being selected (see, for example, Friedman 1953) needs substantial modification in the presence of recognized complexities of the evolutionary process.

groups intermediate between oneself and all – such as class, community or occupation groups – provide the focus of many actions involving committed behaviour. The members of each group may have partly congruent and partly conflicting interests. Actions based on group loyalty may involve, in some respects, a sacrifice of purely personal interests, just as they can also facilitate, in other respects, a greater fulfilment of personal interests. The relative balance of the two may vary. The congruent elements may be more dominant in, say, collusive action on the part of pressure groups agitating for concessions that help the interests of all the members,[17] even though many agitators may also be willing to sacrifice some *personal* gains for the 'cause' of the group. In other relations, e.g. in many cases of family obligations, the extent of sacrifice could indeed be very large.[18] The mixture of selfish and selfless behaviour is one of the important characteristics of group loyalty, and this mixture can be seen in a wide variety of group associations varying from kinship relations and communities to trade unions and economic pressure groups.[19]

---

[17] See, for example, Aumann and Kurz (1977), Becker (1983), Lindbeck (1985). See also Frey (1983).

[18] Traditional family relations in many societies have called for asymmetric sacrifices by some members of the family, e.g. women. The survival of these traditions have often been helped by the acceptance of a particular type of 'ethic' in which gross inequalities in living standards may not appear unacceptable and sometimes may not in fact be consciously recognised and presented for assessment and acceptance. The issue of perception is a central one in understanding sex bias in traditional societies, and an ethical challenge to the traditional moralities call for some cognitive arguments. I have tried to discuss these interrelated factual and moral issues, mainly in the light of Indian evidence, in Sen (1984a, 1985b, 1985f); see also Kynch and Sen (1983).

[19] The so-called 'Japanese ethos' (Morishima 1982; Dore 1983) reflects a

It is important to distinguish between two different issues in the problem of self-interested behaviour. There is, first, the question whether people *actually* behave in an exclusively self-interested way. There is a second question: If people behaved in an exclusively self-interested way, would they achieve certain specified successes, e.g. efficiency of one kind or another?[20] Both these propositions have been attributed to Adam Smith.[21] In fact, however, there is little evidence that he believed in either proposition, contrary to the constant references to the 'Smithian' view on the ubiquity and efficiency of self-interested behaviour. The issue is worth discussing both because Smith was such a

---

special case of group-loyalty of a kind that can be seen to a smaller or larger extent in many types of economic activities involving team work by several people.

[20] The two main definitions of efficiency used in economics are respectively: (1) 'technical efficiency', requiring that no more of any output can be produced without producing less of some other output (treating inputs as negative outputs); and (2) 'economic efficiency', identified with 'Pareto optimality', which requires that no one can be made better off without making someone else worse off. In Chapter 2 the idea of 'economic efficiency' is critically examined.

[21] The latter is the subject of Stephen Leacock's cheerful limerick:

'Adam, Adam, Adam Smith
Listen what I charge you with!
Didn't you say
In the class one day
That selfishness was bound to pay?
Of all doctrines that was the Pith,
Wasn't it, wasn't it, wasn't it, Smith?'
                (Stephen Leacock, *Hellements of Hickonomics*, New York: Dodd,
                                                                Mead & Co., 1936, p. 75)

I am most grateful to Professor Elspeth Rostow for drawing my attention to this forceful presentation of a common interpretation of Adam Smith.

central figure in the origin of economics *and* also because his treatment of the problem is, in fact, illuminating and useful.

Adam Smith and Self-interest

In his enjoyable essay on 'Smith's Travel on the Ship of the State', George Stigler begins with interpreting Smith's remark that 'although the principles of common *prudence* do not always govern the conduct of every individual, they always influence that of the majority of every class or order', as implying: '*self-interest* dominates the majority of men'.[22] In fact, it is not accurate to identify 'prudence' with 'self-interest'. As Smith explains in *The Theory of Moral Sentiments*, prudence is 'the union of' the two qualities of 'reason and understanding', on the one hand, and 'self-command' on the other (Smith, 1790, p. 189). The notion of 'self-command', which Smith took from the Stoics,[23] is not in any sense identical with 'self-interest' or what Smith called 'self-love'.

Indeed, the Stoic roots of Smith's understanding of 'moral sentiments' also make it clear why both sympathy and self-discipline played such an important part in Smith's conception of good behaviour.[24] As Smith himself puts it, 'man, according to the Stoics, ought to regard himself, not as something separated and detached, but as a citizen of the world, a member of the vast commonwealth of nature',

---

[22] Stigler (1975, p. 237); italics added.

[23] On the influence of Stoic thinkers on Adam Smith, see Raphael and Macfie (1976, pp. 5–11), and of course Smith's (1790) own extensive references to the Stoic literature.

[24] On the crucial role of self-discipline, particularly in the suppression of emotions, in the Stoic approach to ethics, see Nussbaum (1986b).

and 'to the interest of this great community, he ought at all times to be willing that his own little interest should be sacrificed' (p. 140). Even though prudence goes well beyond self-interest maximization, Smith saw it in general only as being 'of all virtues that which is most helpful to the individual', whereas 'humanity, justice, generosity, and public spirit, are the qualities most useful to others' (Smith, 1790, p. 189).

It is instructive to examine how it is that Smith's championing of 'sympathy', in addition to 'prudence' (including 'self-command'), has tended to be so lost in the writings of many economists championing the so-called 'Smithian' position on self-interest and its achievements. It is certainly true that Smith saw, as indeed anybody would, that many of our actions are, in fact, guided by self-interest, and some of them do indeed produce good results. One of the passages of Adam Smith that has been quoted again and again by the latter-day Smithians is the following: 'It is not from the benevolence of the butcher, the brewer, or the baker, that we expect our dinner, but from their regard to their own interest. We address ourselves, not to their humanity but to their self-love, and never talk to them of our own necessities but of their advantages' (Smith, 1776, pp. 26–7).

While many admirers of Smith do not seem to have gone beyond this bit about the butcher and the brewer, a reading of even this passage would indicate that what Smith is doing here is to specify why and how normal transactions in the market are carried out, and why and how division of labour works, which is the subject of the chapter in which the quoted passage occurs. But the fact that Smith noted that mutually advantageous trades are very common does not indicate at all that he thought self-love alone, or indeed prudence broadly construed, could be adequate for a good society. Indeed, he maintained precisely the opposite. He did not rest economic salvation on some unique motivation.

In fact, Smith chastised Epicurus for trying to see virtue entirely in terms of prudence, and Smith seized the occasion to rap 'philosophers' on their knuckles for trying to reduce everything to some one virtue:

> By running up all the different virtues too to this one species of propriety, Epicurus indulged in a propensity which is natural to all men, but which philosophers in particular are apt to cultivate with a peculiar fondness, as the great means of displaying their ingenuity, the propensity to account for all appearances from as few principles as possible.
>
> (Smith 1790, p. 299)

It is a matter of some irony, that this 'peculiar fondness' would be attributed to Smith himself by his overenthusiastic admirers in making him the 'guru' of self-interest (contrary to what he actually said).[25]

Smith's attitude to 'self-love' has something in common with that of Edgeworth, who thought that 'economical calculus' as opposed to ethical evaluation, was particularly relevant to two specific activities, to wit, 'war and contract'.[26] The reference to contract is of course precisely similar to Smith's reference to trade, because trade takes

---

[25] I have discussed the nature of this misrepresentation in a paper called 'Adam Smith's Prudence', Sen (1986b). See also Winch (1978) and Brennan and Lomasky (1986). On related matters, see Hollander (1973), Raphael (1985), Skinner and Wilson (1975), Rosenberg (1984).

[26] Edgeworth (1881, p. 52). As a good utilitarian Edgeworth refers only to utilitarianism as a possible ethical approach, but his general contrast between self-interested and ethical calculations is clear enough. See also Collard (1975).

place on the basis of mutually advantageous (explicit or implicit) contracts. But there are many other activities inside economics and outside it in which the simple pursuit of self-interest is not the great redeemer, and Smith did not assign a generally superior role to the pursuit of self-interest in any of his writings. The defence of self-interested behaviour comes in specific contexts, particularly related to various contemporary bureaucratic barriers and other restrictions to economic transactions which made trade difficult and hampered production.[27]

One specific field in which Smith's economic analysis has been widely misinterpreted with grave consequences is that of famine and starvation. This issue relates to the place of the profit motive only indirectly. Smith did argue that though traders are often blamed for causing famines, they do not in fact cause them, and famines usually follow from what he called 'a real scarcity' (Smith, 1776, p. 526). He was opposed to suppressing or restricting trade. But this did not imply that he was against public support for the poor. Indeed unlike Malthus, Smith was not opposed to

---

[27] Smith emphasized very clearly the contemporary nature of many of his concerns. Indeed, he seemed to have been clinically concerned that the temporal context of his remarks should not be misunderstood. In fact, the 'Advertisement' for the third edition of the *Wealth of Nations*, was almost entirely devoted to clarifying the temporal context of his reference to 'the present state of things': 'The First Edition of the following Work was printed in the end of the year 1775, and in the beginning of the year 1776. Through the greater part of the Book, therefore, whenever the present state of things is mentioned, it is to be understood of the state they were in, either about that time or at some earlier period, during the time I was employed in writing the book. To this third Edition, however, I have made several additions . . . In all these additions, *the present state of things* means always the state in which they were during the year 1783 and the beginning of the present year 1784' (in the edition of Campbell and Skinner, Smith 1776, p. 8).

Poor Laws, though he did criticize it for the harshness and counterproductive nature of some of the restrictive rules affecting the beneficiaries (pp. 152–4).

Furthermore, in the *Wealth of Nations*, Smith did also discuss the possibility of famines arising from an economic process involving the market mechanism, without being caused by 'a real scarcity' generated by a decline in food output as such.[28]

> But it would be otherwise in a country where the funds destined for the maintenance of labour were sensibly decaying. Every year the demand for servants and labourers would, in all the different classes of employments, be less than it had the year before. Many who had been bred in the superior classes, not being able to find employment in their own business, would be glad to seek it in the lowest. The lowest class being not only overstocked with its own workmen, but with the overflowings of all the other classes, the competition for employment would be so great in it, as to reduce the wages of labour to the most miserable and scanty subsistence of the labourer. Many would not be able to find employment even upon these hard terms, but would either starve, or be driven to seek a subsistence either by begging, or by the perpetration perhaps of the greatest enormities. Want, famine, and mortality would immediately prevail in that class, and from then on extend themselves to all the superior classes.
>
> (Smith 1776, pp. 90–1)

In this analysis, people are led to starvation and famine

---

[28] Smith's complex views on the causation of famines have been discussed in Sen (1986a).

through a process over which they themselves have little control. While Smith was often cited by imperial administrators for justification of refusing to intervene in famines in such diverse places as Ireland, India and China, there is nothing to indicate that Smith's ethical approach to public policy would have precluded intervention in support of the entitlements of the poor. Even though he would have certainly been opposed to the suppression of trade, his pointer to unemployment and low real wages as causes of starvation suggests a variety of public policy responses.[29]

The misinterpretation of Smith's complex attitude to motivation and markets, and the neglect of his ethical

---

[29] It can be argued that a person's failure to acquire enough food can be either due to 'pull failure' (e.g arising from a fall in income related to becoming unemployed or a decline in real wages) or due to 'response failure' (e.g. the traders manipulate the market in such a way that the demand is not properly met and instead a lot of profits are made by cornering the market). It is clear from Smith's analysis of famines that he did not dispute the possibility of starvation arising from 'pull failure', but he did reject the plausibility of 'response failure'. It is, thus, arguable that the real 'Smithian' message regarding anti-famine policy is not non-action, but creation of entitlements of victim groups through supplementary income generation, leaving the market to respond to the demand resulting from the generated incomes of the would-be victim groups. This analysis has a good deal of bearing on policy debates that are taking place now, and suggests a more production-oriented policy (not just of food but also of other commodities that could be exchanged for food) rather than pure relief. As far as short-run relief is concerned, it suggests the case for greater reliance on cash relief at the place of normal work and living, combined with adding to food supply in the market, rather than the state trying to deal with the logistic problem of getting both the victims and the food to hastily constructed relief camps. In judging the merits and demerits of these various policy alternatives, Smith's analysis remains relevant and important. I have discussed these policy options (and the relevance of Smith's economic analysis to current-day debates) in Sen (1986a).

analysis of sentiments and behaviour, fits well into the distancing of economics from ethics that has occurred with the development of modern economics. Smith did, in fact, make pioneering contributions in analysing the nature of mutually advantageous exchanges, and the value of division of labour, and since these contributions are perfectly consistent with human behaviour *sans* bonhomie and ethics, references to these parts of Smith's work have been profuse and exuberant. Other parts of Smith's writings on economics and society, dealing with observations of misery, the need for sympathy, and the role of ethical considerations in human behaviour, particularly the use of behaviour norms, have become relatively neglected as these considerations have themselves become unfashionable in economics.

The support that believers in, and advocates of, self-interested behaviour have sought in Adam Smith is, in fact, hard to find on a wider and less biased reading of Smith. The professor of moral philosophy and the pioneer economist did not, in fact, lead a life of spectacular schizophrenia. Indeed, it is precisely the narrowing of the broad Smithian view of human beings, in modern economies, that can be seen as one of the major deficiencies of contemporary economic theory. This impoverishment is closely related to the distancing of economics from ethics. In the third lecture I shall pursue this question further.

Another serious consequence of this distancing is a weakening of the reach and relevance of welfare economics itself. That is the subject of the second lecture.

2 Economic Judgements and Moral Philosophy

The position of welfare economics in modern economic theory has been a rather precarious one. In classical political economy there were no sharp boundaries drawn between welfare economic analysis and other types of economic investigation. But as the suspicion of the use of ethics in economics has grown, welfare economics has appeared to be increasingly dubious. It has been put into an arbitrarily narrow box, separated from the rest of economics. Contact with the outside world has been mainly in the form of a one-way relationship by which findings of predictive economics are allowed to influence welfare economic analysis, but welfare economic ideas are not allowed to influence predictive economics, since actual human action is taken to be based on self-interest only, without any impact of ethical considerations or of welfare–economic judgements. For example, ideas about the response of labour to wage incentives are brought into welfare–economic analysis of, say, wages policy or optimum taxation, but welfare–economic ideas are not permitted to affect the behaviour of workers and thus influence the incentive problem itself. Welfare economics has been something like an economic equivalent of the 'black hole' – things can get into it, but nothing can escape from it.

Interpersonal Comparisons of Utility

The standard propositions of modern welfare economics depend on combining self-seeking behaviour, on the one hand, and judging social achievement by some utility-based criterion on the other. In fact, the traditional welfare economic criterion used to be the simple utilitarian one, judging success by the size of the *sum total* of utility created – nothing else being taken to be of intrinsic value. As ethical analysis goes, this is pretty straight and narrow, but that side of the story was narrowed even further, as interpersonal comparisons of utility came under fire in the 1930s, led by Lionel Robbins (1935, 1938).

For reasons that are not altogether clear, interpersonal utility comparisons were then diagnosed as being themselves 'normative' or 'ethical'.[1] It is, of course, possible to argue that interpersonal comparisons of utility make no sense and are indeed totally meaningless – a position I find hard to defend,[2] but certainly have no difficulty in

---

[1] The popularity of that view is perhaps traceable to the powerful endorsement of that position by Lionel Robbins (1935, 1938), in particular passages, such as the following: 'The theory of exchange does *not* assume that, at any point, it is necessary to compare the satisfaction which *I* get from the spending of 6d. on bread with the satisfaction which *the Baker* gets by receiving it. That comparison is a comparison of an entirely different nature. . . . It involves an element of conventional valuation. Hence it is essentially normative' (pp. 138–9). It is, however, arguable that Robbins was really more concerned with establishing the negative proposition that interpersonal comparisons cannot be made 'scientifically' than with asserting the positive claim that such comparisons are 'normative' or 'ethical'. On the nature of 'normative' comparisons of utility (in particular, its dependence on some specific 'norm' or view of the 'good'), see Sen (1982a, Essays 12 and 19).

[2] On this question, see Harsanyi (1955), Graaff (1957), Little (1957);

understanding. If that position were accepted, then the statement that person A is happier than B would be nonsensical – *ethical* nonsense just as much as it would be *descriptive* nonsense. I guess it is a reflection of the way ethics tends to be viewed by economists that statements suspected of being 'meaningless' or 'nonsensical' are promptly taken to be 'ethical'. The peculiarly narrow view of 'meaning' championed by logical positivists – enough to cause disorder in philosophy itself – caused total chaos in welfare economics when it was supplemented by some additional home-grown confusions liberally supplied by economists themselves. Positivist philosophers may have been off beam in taking all ethical propositions to be meaningless, but even they had not suggested that all meaningless propositions were ethical!

Pareto Optimality and Economic Efficiency

Be that as it may, with the development of anti-ethicalism, as interpersonal comparisons of utility were eschewed in welfare economics, the surviving criterion was that of Pareto optimality. A social state is described as Pareto optimal if and only if no-one's utility can be raised without reducing the utility of someone else. This is a very limited

---

Suppes (1966, 1969), Van Praag (1968, 1971, 1978), Jeffrey (1971), Van Praag and Kapteyn (1973), Hammond (1977), Ng (1979), Sen (1979c), Hare (1981), Griffin (1982), Suzumura (1983), Kaneko (1984), Nozick (1985), Davidson (1986), Gibbard (1986). Interpersonal comparability need not take an 'all or nothing' form. Various structures and interpretations of partial interpersonal comparability can be found in Sen (1970a, 1970b), Blackorby (1975), Fine (1975a), Basu (1979), Bezembinder and Van Acker (1986). See also Levi (1974) on the comparable problem of 'indeterminate probabilities'.

kind of success, and in itself may or may not guarantee much. A state can be Pareto optimal with some people in extreme misery and others rolling in luxury, so long as the miserable cannot be made better off without cutting into the luxury of the rich.[3] Pareto optimality can, like 'Caesar's spirit', 'come hot from hell'.

Pareto optimality is sometimes also called 'economic efficiency'. That usage is appropriate from one point of

---

[3] There has, however, been a considerable revival of interest in recent years in distributional questions related to normative analysis of inequality; see especially Atkinson (1970, 1975, 1983). See also Fisher (1956), Aigner and Heins (1967), Theil (1967), Kolm (1969, 1976), Bentzel (1970), Newbery (1970), Tinbergen (1970), Pen (1971), Sheshinski (1972), Dasgupta, Sen and Starrett (1973), Rothschild and Stiglitz (1973), Sen (1973b, 1976b, 1982a), Muellbauer (1974, 1978), Blackorby and Donaldson (1977, 1978, 1984), Hammond (1976b, 1977, 1978), Meade (1976), Mehran (1976), Pyatt (1976, 1985), Bhattacharya and Chatterjee (1977), Cowell (1977), Graaff (1977), Hansson (1977), Fields and Fei (1978), Kern (1978), Archibald and Donaldson (1979), Bourguignon (1979), Dutta (1980), Deaton and Muellbauer (1980), Kakwani (1980b, 1981, 1986), Roberts (1980c), Shorrocks (1980, 1983, 1984), Nygard and Sandstrom (1981), Atkinson and Bourguignon (1982), Broder and Morris (1982), Mookherjee and Shorrocks (1982), Osmani (1982), Anand (1983), Eichorn and Gehrig (1983), Jorgenson and Slesnick (1984a,b), Le Grand (1984), Ebert (1985), Le Breton, Trannoy, and Uriarte (1985), Shorrocks and Foster (1985), Foster (1986), Kanbur and Stromberg (1986), Maasoumi (1986), Temkin (1986), among other contributions. There is also a related literature on the measurement of poverty, paying particular attention to the assessment of inequality involved *inter alia* in the exercise; see Sen (1976a, 1981a, 1982a), Anand (1977, 1983), Taylor (1977) Ahluwalia (1978), Dutta (1978), Hamada and Takayama (1978), Takayama (1979), Thon (1979), Blackory and Donaldson (1980), Fields (1980), Kakwani (1980a,b, 1986), Clark, Hemming and Ulph (1981), Srinivasan (1981), Streeten (1981a), Osmani (1982), Kundu and Smith (1983), Foster, Greer and Thorbecke (1984), Chakravarty (1983a,b), Foster (1984), Lipton (1985), Bigman (1986), Donaldson and Weymark (1986), Jorgenson and Slesnick (1986), Seidl (1986), among others.

view, in that Pareto optimality deals exclusively with efficiency in the space of utilities, paying no attention to the distributional considerations regarding utility. However, in another respect the term is unfortunate, since the whole focus of analysis here continues to be utility, and this is a legacy left by the earlier utilitarian tradition. It is, of course, possible to introduce *other* considerations in judging the success of persons and thus of the society (see, for example, Rawls 1971, 1980, 1982). Pareto optimality captures the efficiency aspects only of utility-based accounting. I shall have to come back to this question presently, but for the moment I want to follow further the story of the narrowing of welfare economics.[4]

In the small box to which welfare economics got

---

[4] One way of extending Paretian welfare economics without introducing any interpersonal comparisons is to use a 'compensation test'. It has been proposed that the possibility of the gainers being able to overcompensate the losers may be seen as a social improvement (see Kaldor 1939 and Hicks 1939). Such criteria of social improvement lead to inconsistencies (on this see Scitovsky 1941, Samuelson 1950, Gorman 1955). But this is only one problem with compensation criteria. Another – arguably more basic – difficulty relates to the question as to why the mere *possibility* of compensating the losers should be adequate to establish a social improvement even if the compensation is not, *in fact*, to be paid. The losers could include the worst off and the most miserable in the society, and it is little consolation to be told that it is possible to compensate them fully, but ('good God!') no actual plan to do so. If, on the other hand, the losers are *in fact* compensated, then the overall outcome – after compensation – is a Pareto improvement, and then there is no *need* for the compensation test as a supplement to the Pareto principle. So the compensation criteria are either *unconvincing* or *redundant*. The Pareto principle can scarcely be extended to cover judgements of distribution without actually making interpersonally comparative distributional judgements (on which see Little 1957, Phelps 1973, Meade 1976, Ng 1979).

confined, with Pareto optimality as the only criterion of judgement, and self-seeking behaviour as the only basis of economic choice, the scope for saying something interesting in welfare economics became exceedingly small.[5] One important proposition in this small territory is the so-called 'Fundamental Theorem of Welfare Economics', which relates the results of market equilibrium under perfect competition with Pareto optimality. It shows that under certain conditions (in particular, no 'externality', i.e. no interdependences that are external to the market), every perfectly competitive equilibrium is Pareto optimal, and with some other conditions (in particular no economies of large scale), every Pareto optimal social state is also a perfectly competitive equilibrium, with respect to some set of prices (and for some initial distribution of people's endowments).[6] This is a remarkably elegant result, and one that also gives some deep insights into the nature of the

---

[5] Arrow's (1951a, 1963) 'impossibility theorem' brings out, in a dramatic way, the tension involved in ruling out the use of interpersonal comparisons of utility, in aggregating individual preferences into consistent and complete social choice, satisfying some mild-looking conditions of reasonableness. There is an enormous literature, following Arrow's lead, devoted to discussing the significance of Arrow's result, seeking ways out of the impossibility, extending that impossibility, and investigating related issues. On the nature of the various problems involved, see Hansson (1968), Sen (1980a, 1986e), Pattanaik (1971, 1978), Fishburn (1973), Brown (1976), Plott (1976), Gottinger and Leinfellner (1978), Kelly (1978), Pollak (1979), Blair and Pollak (1983), Chichilnisky and Heal (1983), Moulin (1983), Pattanaik and Salles (1983), Suzumura (1983), Dummett (1984), Peleg (1984), Hurley (1985b), Nitzan and Paroush (1985), Elster and Hylland (1986), Schwartz (1986), among others.

[6] See Arrow (1951b), Debreu (1959), and McKenzie (1959). See also Malinvaud (1961). An excellent general account can be found in Arrow and Hahn (1971). For the bearing of this result, and related ones, on various branches of welfare economics, see Ng (1979) and Boadway and Bruce (1984).

working of the price mechanism, explaining the mutually advantageous nature of trade, production and consumption geared to the pursuit of self-interest. One significant aspect of economic relationships pursued through the market mechanism got sorted out by this result and related ones.

Despite its general importance, the ethical content of this welfare economic result is, however, rather modest. The criterion of Pareto optimality is an extremely limited way of assessing social achievement, so that the part of the result which claims that a perfectly competitive equilibrium, under the specified conditions, must be Pareto optimal, is correspondingly limited. The converse proposition, i.e. that every Pareto optimal social state is a perfectly competitive equilibrium for some initial distribution of endowments, is more appealing, because it has been thought reasonable to suppose that the very best state must be *at least* Pareto optimal, so that the very best state too must be achievable through the competitive mechanism. Various procedures for supplementing the Pareto principle by distributional judgements have been considered (see, for example, Fisher 1956, Little 1957, Fisher and Rothenberg 1961, Kolm 1969, Phelps 1973, 1977, Meade 1976, Sen 1976b, 1979c, Hammond 1978, Ng 1979, Roberts 1980b, Atkinson and Bourguignon 1982, Osmani 1982, Atkinson 1983, Jorgenson and Slesnick (1984a, 1984b), Yaari and Bar-Hilell (1984), Maasoumi 1986).[7]

---

[7] One interesting and important approach of supplementing Pareto optimality through distributional judgements involves the criterion of 'fairness', which demands that nobody envies the commodity bundle enjoyed by another. There is an extensive literature using this approach (see Foley 1967, Schmeidler and Vind 1972, Feldman and Kirman 1974, Pazner and Schmeidler 1974, Varian 1974, 1975, Svensson 1977, 1985, Feldman 1980, Suzumura 1983, among other contributions). Note that non-envy can coexist with great inequalities of well-being, since the comparisons are 'situational' rather than 'comprehensive', in that interpersonal variations of well-being functions

However, part of the difficulty[8] in applying this result for public action arises from the fact that the information needed to calculate the required initial distribution of endowments is exacting and very hard to get, and individuals may not have the incentive to reveal the necessary information. While the competitive market mechanism itself ensures an economy of information as far as the decisions of *individual agents* are concerned (given the initial distribution), the informational requirements for *public* decisions regarding initial ownerships cannot be easily obtained through any simple mechanism.[9]

Given self-interested behaviour, the market mechanism

---

are not considered. If $W_1(x)$ and $W_2(x)$ are the well-being functions respectively of persons 1 and 2, and $W_1(x_2) > W_1(x_1) > W_2(x_2) > W_2(x_1)$, when x_1 and x_2 are the bundles respectively enjoyed by persons 1 and 2, then it is person 1 who envies person's 2's bundle while person 2 has no such envy, even though it is person 2 who is clearly worse off in terms of well-being than person 1. Further, if we have $W_1(x_1) > W_1(x_2) > W_2(x_2) > W_2(x_1)$, then the condition of 'non-envy' is completely satisfied on both sides, even though person 2 is clearly worse off then person 1. Since economic misfortunes are often associated with variations in the well-being functions, due to such factors as disability, illness, age, social discrimination, etc., there is much scope for doubting the fairness of the fairness criterion.

[8] A more obvious problem relates to the exacting nature of the assumptions required for the relationship to hold, e.g. the absence of externalities and of increasing returns to scale (except of particularly limited types). The restrictive nature of the traditional format of resource allocation has been brought out particularly clearly in the recent years by the greater recognition of the importance of environmental considerations and of natural resources (see Bohm and Kneese 1971, Mäler 1974, Dasgupta and Heal 1979, Dasgupta 1982a).

[9] Recently the 'Fundamental Theorem of Welfare Economics' has been extended to cover public goods as well, i.e. those goods for which the consumption of one person does not reduce the consumption of another (e.g. the use of an uncrowded public park; see Green and

provides good incentives for every agent to choose appropriately, *given* his initial endowments, but there is no comparable mechanism by which people have the incentive to reveal the information on the basis of which the choice *among* Pareto optimal states could be made and the appropriate initial distribution could be fixed. The usual mechanisms of decentralized resource allocation are also of no use in getting the necessary background information, since they act on the basis of 'team work' on the part of the different agents involved, whereas distributional decisions involve conflict between one agent and another. Thus, the ground that can be covered for actual action on the basis of the second part of the 'fundamental theorem' is rather limited.

There is a further problem that even if such information were available, the second part of the 'fundamental theorem' would be used only if it were politically possible to redistribute resources among the people in any way that would be required by considerations of social optimality. Even if the necessary lump-sum transfers were identifiable and also economically feasible, issues of political feasibility can be, obviously, extremely important when dealing with such fundamental matters as radical changes in ownership. Even though the invoking of the second part of the 'fundamental theorem' may often come from rather conservative quarters defending the market mechanism,

---

Laffont (1979), Groves and Ledyard (1977), and Dasgupta, Hammond and Maskin (1979)). This is a remarkable achievement, but it must be recognized that this class of results have exactly similar problems to the original efficiency results regarding the information needed for public decisions about choosing the appropriate initial distribution of endowments. On related matters, see Gibbard (1973), Satterthwaite (1975), Pattanaik (1978), Schmeidler and Sonnenschein (1978), Laffont (1979), Moulin (1983), Peleg (1984).

that result can be of real use only as a part of some 'revolutionary's handbook', transforming the ownership of means of production before getting the market to do the rest. If radical redistributions of ownership were not possible, movements towards overall social optimality will require mixed mechanisms of a kind not covered by the 'fundamental theorem'.

Utility, Pareto Optimality and Welfarism

There is one other respect in which the significance of the 'fundamental theorem' needs some clarification. The idea that overall social optimality must *inter alia* require Pareto optimality is based on the notion that if a change is advantageous for each, then it must be a good change for the society. That notion must in some sense be correct, but to identify advantage with utility is far from obvious. And if, in contrast, some interpretation of advantage other than utility is accepted, then Pareto optimality – defined as it is in terms of individual utilities – would lose its status of being even a *necessary* condition, if not sufficient, for overall social optimality.

The enormous standing of Pareto optimality in welfare economics, as was argued earlier, relates closely to the hallowed position of utilitarianism in traditional welfare economics (before questions were raised about the possibility of interpersonal comparisons of utility). If interpersonal comparisons of utility are dropped, but nevertheless utility is regarded as the only thing of intrinsic value, then Pareto optimality would be the natural surviving criterion, since it carries the utilitarian logic as far forward as possible without actually making any interpersonal comparisons of utility. In fact, it can be easily shown that the utilitarian criterion when combined with entirely non-comparable utilities will yield a partial ordering of unambiguous social rankings, and that partial ordering will coincide exactly with the social ranking achieved by the Pareto criterion.[10] Utilitarianism as a moral principle can be seen to be a combination of three more elementary requirements:

1 *'welfarism'*, requiring that the goodness of a state of affairs be a function only of the utility information regarding that state;
2 *'sum-ranking'*, requiring that utility information regarding any state be assessed by looking only at the sum-total of all the utilities in that state;
3 *'consequentialism'*, requiring that every choice, whether of actions, institutions, motivations, rules, etc., be ultimately determined by the goodness of the consequent states of affairs.

On its own, the Pareto criterion can be seen as capturing a particular aspect of welfarism, to wit: a unanimous ranking of individual utilities must be adequate for overall social ranking of the respective states.[11] In fact, the policy use of the Pareto criterion goes beyond welfarism and embraces consequentialism as well, since choices of actions, institutions, etc. are all required to satisfy Pareto optimality, so that consequentialism is implicitly but firmly demanded.

---

[10] These and related propositions can be found in Sen (1970a), Chapter 7. See also Blackorby and Donaldson (1977) and Wittman (1984).

[11] In fact, welfarism can be effectively derived from the Pareto principle and a combination of Arrow's independence condition and unrestricted domain, applied to a framework with or without interpersonal comparisons of utility (see Guha 1972, Blau 1976, d'Aspremont and Gevers 1977, Deschamps and Gevers 1978, Sen 1977b, 1979a, Gevers 1979, Roberts 1980a, d'Aspremont 1985).

I leave for the moment the question of the status of Pareto optimality, and take up some general issues regarding the acceptability of welfarism.[12] Welfarism is the view that the only things of intrinsic value for ethical calculation and evaluation of states of affairs are individual utilities.[13]

Well-being and Agency

It is useful to distinguish between two different criticisms that can be made of welfarism, and in particular of taking utility to be the only source of value. First, it can be argued that utility is, at best, a reflection of a person's well-being, but the person's success cannot be judged exclusively in terms of his or her well-being (even if social success is

---

[12] On this, see also Sen (1970a, 1979b), Williams (1973a, 1981), Scanlon (1975, 1982), Broome (1978), Dworkin (1978, 1981), Slote (1983, 1985), Parfit (1984), Gauthier (1986), among other critiques.

[13] Utilities can, of course, be defined in many different ways (see Ramsey 1931, Pigou 1952, Harsanyi 1955, Gosling 1969, Starr 1973, Hare 1981, Griffin 1982, 1986, Hammond 1982, Mirrlees 1982). The richness of the utilitarian perspective relates to this versatility. However, some defenders of utility-based calculation seem to have been tempted to redefine the term 'utility' to cover whatever it is that we wish to value. As a defence of utility-based ethical calculation this is tautologous and adds little to the discussion. However, 'utility' can serve as a convenient short-hand for well-being, without much commitment specifically to the metric of happiness, or desire-fulfilment (see, for example, Hammond 1982).It is in this general form that the term has been used in axiomatic derivations of various well-being-based rules in a framework of 'social welfare functionals' (see, for example, Sen 1970a, 1977b, Hammond 1976a, Strasnick 1976, Arrow 1977, d'Aspremont and Gevers 1977, Deschamps and Gevers 1978, Maskin 1978, Gevers 1979, Roberts 1980a, Myerson 1983, Blackorby, Donaldson and Weymark 1984, d'Aspremont 1985).

judged entirely by the constituent individual successes). A person may value the promotion of certain causes and the occurrence of certain things, even though the importance that is attached to these developments are not reflected by the advancement of his or her well-being, if any, that they respectively cause. Second, it can be disputed that personal well-being is best seen as utility rather than in some other terms. I discuss the former point first.

I have tried to argue elsewhere (Sen 1985a) that there is an essential and irreducible 'duality' in the conception of a person in ethical calculation. We can see the person, in terms of *agency*, recognizing and respecting his or her ability to form goals, commitments, values, etc., and we can also see the person in terms of *well-being*, which too calls for attention. This dichotomy is lost in a model of exclusively self-interested motivation, in which a person's agency must be entirely geared to his own well-being. But once that straitjacket of self-interested motivation is removed, it becomes possible to give recognition to the indisputable fact that the person's agency can well be geared to considerations not covered – or at least not *fully* covered – by his or her own well-being.

Valuing and Value

It might be asked whether attaching importance to each person's agency would amount to taking a 'subjectivist' view of ethics, since whatever a person values and wishes to achieve might have to be, then, taken as valuable precisely because he or she values it. But, in fact, the controversial issue of objectivity (on which see, among other contributions, Scanlon 1975, Mackie 1978, Nagel 1980, 1986, McDowell 1981, 1985, Hurley 1985a, 1985b, Sen 1985a, 1986f, Wiggins 1985, Williams 1985) is not foreclosed by taking agency as important.

This is so for two distinct reasons. First, to attach importance to the agency aspect of each person does not entail accepting whatever a person happens to value as being valuable (i) unconditionally, and (ii) as intensely as it is valued by the person. Respecting the agency aspect points to the appropriateness of going beyond a person's well-being into his or her valuations, commitments, etc., but the necessity of assessing these valuations, commitments, etc. is not eliminated by the mere acceptance of that appropriateness. Agency may be seen as important (not just instrumentally for the pursuit of well-being, but also intrinsically), but that still leaves open the question as to how that agency is to be evaluated and appraised. I have tried to argue elsewhere (Sen 1985a) that even though 'the use of one's agency is, in an important sense, a matter for oneself to judge', 'the need for careful assessment of aims, objective, allegiances, etc., and of the conception of the good, may be important and exacting' (p. 203). The issue of objectivity relates to the interpretation of that 'careful assessment' – as to what *kind* of an exercise it is taken to be.

Second, it is also the case that an objectivist second-order view of ethics can co-exist with a substantive ethics that includes among the valuable objects people's ability to get what they do, in fact, value. Getting (or having the capability of getting) what one values is not, in this respect, particularly different from other things that might be valued, e.g. happiness, well-being, liberty, and it can thus figure in an objectivist valuation function in much the same way as these other objects might figure in such a function. The issue of foundation has to be distinguished from the nature of the objects that are valued. Even an objectively founded theory can give an important role to what people actually do value and to their ability to get those things.[14]

---

[14] I have discussed this question more extensively in the introduction to

Agency and Well-being: Distinction and
Interdependence

To recognize the distinction between the 'agency aspect'
and the 'well-being aspect' of a person does not require us
to take the view that the person's success as an agent must
be independent, or completely separable from, his success
in terms of well-being. A person may well feel happier and
better off as a result of achieving what he wanted to
achieve – perhaps for his family, or his community, or his
class, or his party, or some other cause. Also it is quite
possible that a person's well-being will go down as a result
of frustration if there is some failure to achieve what he
wanted to achieve as an agent, even though those
achievements are not directly concerned with his well-
being. There is really no sound basis for demanding that
the agency aspect and the well-being aspect of a person
should be independent of each other, and it is, I suppose,
even possible that every change in one will affect the other
as well. However, the point at issue is not the plausibility of
their *independence*, but the sustainability and relevance of
the *distinction*. The fact that two variables may be so
related that one cannot change without the other, does not
imply that they are the same variable, or that they will have
the same values, or even that the value of one can be
obtained from the other on the basis of some simple
transformation.

The importance of an agency achievement does not rest
entirely on the enhancement of well-being that it may
indirectly cause. For example, if one fights hard for the

the book version of my Dewey Lectures (and other essays), *Well-*
being, Agency and Freedom to be published by Blackwell and
Columbia University Press.

independence of one's country, and when that independence is achieved, one happens also to feel happier, the
main achievement is that of independence, of which the
happiness at that achievement is only one consequence.It is
not unnatural to be happy at that achievement, but the
achievement does not consist only of that happiness. It is,
therefore, plausible to argue that the agency achievement
and well-being achievement, both of which have some
distinct importance, may be causally linked with each
other, but this fact does not compromise the specific
importance of either. In so far as utility-based welfarist
calculus concentrates only on the well-being of the person,[15] ignoring the agency aspect, or actually fails to

---

[15] Though utility is typically interpreted in terms of well-being, it is
possible to argue that it might be better seen as reflecting a person's
agency. That argument is particularly difficult for the 'happiness' or
'pleasure-pain' interpretation of utility, and it is not easy for the
'desire-fulfilment' interpretation either. But the 'choice' interpretation
may offer more immediate scope for being taken as standing for the
exercise of agency, not necessarily related to well-being. That is not,
of course, the way the choice-interpretation of utility is standardly
viewed (e.g. in 'revealed preference' theory). Indeed, choice is seen as
important in the typical utilitarian perspective precisely because of its
alleged congruence with well-being. But moving away from the
standard view, it is possible to argue that the choice interpretation
may make utility-based calculus more linked with agency than with
well-being, and 'utility' (thus interpreted) can then be valued on
grounds of the importance of agency. However, since the agency
aspects requires careful assessment of values and valuations, the
formula of taking any choice as reflection of valuable agency is plainly
inadequate. Further, the importance of agency may not be entirely
capturable in terms of the promotion of a person's goals and may
require a format that is not as crudely 'maximizing' as the numerical
representation of a choice function has to be (on this see Sen 1982b,
1983c, and also Lecture 3). Nevertheless, this perspective can serve as
the basis of a different interpretation of utility-based ethical

distinguish between the agency aspect and the well-being aspect altogether, something of real importance *is* lost.

Utility and Well-being

The second difficulty with welfarism arises from the particular interpretation of well-being that utility provides. To judge the well-being of a person exclusively in the metric of happiness or desire-fulfilment has some obvious limitations. These limitations are particularly damaging in the context of interpersonal comparisons of well-being, since the extent of happiness reflects what one can expect and how the social 'deal' seems in comparison with that. A person who has had a life of misfortune, with very little opportunities, and rather little hope, may be more easily reconciled to deprivations than others reared in more fortunate and affluent circumstances. The metric of happiness may, therefore, distort the extent of deprivation, in a specific and biased way. The hopeless beggar, the precarious landless labourer, the dominated housewife, the hardened unemployed or the over-exhausted coolie may all take pleasures in small mercies, and manage to suppress intense suffering for the necessity of continuing survival, but it would be ethically deeply mistaken to attach a correspondingly small value to the loss of their well-being

---

accounting. Of course, insofar as utility stands for agency, it cannot at the same time reflect well-being, and there is, thus, no possibility of relying on utility-based calculation – however interpreted – in catching the dual basis of well-being and agency in substantive ethics. The duality between achievement and freedom is also not capturable within the 'monist' framework of utility-based calculus. The informational content of one utility number – no matter how it is translated – is obviously quite limited.

because of this survival strategy. The same problem arises with the other interpretation of utility, namely, desire-fulfilment, since the hopelessly deprived lack the courage to desire much, and their deprivations are muted and deadened in the scale of desire-fulfilment.

This particular problem of influence of contingent circumstances on the metric of utility is only a reflection of a more basic problem, to wit, the insufficient depth of the criterion of happiness or desire-fulfilment in judging a person's well-being. Well-being is ultimately a matter of valuation, and while happiness and the fulfilment of desire may well be valuable for the person's well-being, they cannot – on their own or even together – adequately reflect the value of well-being.[16] 'Being happy' is not even a valuational activity, and 'desiring' is at best a consequence of valuation. The need for valuation in assessing well-being demands a more direct recognition.

It is, therefore, arguable that since the claim of utility to be the only source of value rests allegedly on identifying utility with well-being, it can be criticized both:

1 on the ground that well-being is not the only thing that is valuable;

---

[16] I have discussed these issues in Sen (1980, 1985a), in which I have also explored an alternative conception of well-being in the form of the capability to achieve valuable functionings. This approach, which develops ideas explored earlier by Smith (1776, 1790), and Marx (1844, 1875, 1883), and still earlier by Aristotle (on which see Nussbaum 1986c), involves a number of problems of measurement and weighting, which are difficult but not insurmountable (see Sen 1985b). This way of seeing well-being has powerful implications not only for welfare economics, but also for the assessment of standards of living, poverty, inequality, sexual divisions and social justice (see Sen 1980a, 1982a, 1983d, 1984a, 1984b, 1985b, 1985c, 1985f, 1986e; see also Sen *et al.* (1987), with discussions by Keith Hart, Geoffrey Hawthorn, Ravi Kanbur, John Muellbauer, and Bernard Williams).

2 on the ground that utility does not adequately represent well-being.

In so far as we are concerned with people's achievements, in making ethical judgement, utility achievement may well be partial, inadequate and misleading.[17]

Achievements, Freedom and Rights

There is another – in some sense more basic – question as to whether a person's advantage is best seen in terms of his or her achievement. This issue arises in evaluating both well-being and agency. It can be argued that advantage may be better represented by the freedom that the person has, and not by (at least not entirely by) what the person achieves – in well-being or in terms of agency – on the basis of that freedom. This type of consideration will take us in the direction of rights, liberties, and real opportunities. If in ethical accounting the person's advantages are judged – at least partly – in terms of freedom-type considerations, then not merely utilitarianism and welfarism, but also a

---

[17] I have not considered here explicitly the interpretation of utility in terms of choice. That approach is hard to use as far as interpersonal comparisons of utility are concerned, since people do not actually face the choice of becoming someone else. It is possible to extend the choice framework to interpersonal comparisons (as Vickrey 1945 and Harsanyi 1955 have skilfully done) by posing hypothetical choices regarding becoming one person or another. But the understandability and relevance of such extremely counterfactual choices are far from clear. Furthermore, since the interpretation of choice must at least partly depend on the motivation guiding that choice, it is not clear that there is an immediate and easy translation from choice – irrespective of the underlying motivation – to well-being. See also footnote 15, page 44.

number of other approaches that concentrate on achievement alone would have to be rejected.[18]

In the ethical literature rights-based moral theories go back a long time, and indeed utilitarians like Jeremy Bentham paid a good deal of attention to rejecting such theories, describing the various doctrines as 'simple nonsense', 'bawling upon paper', and 'rhetorical nonsense, nonsense upon stilts'.[19] Rights-based theories have not,

---

[18] Different ways of judging a person's advantage also affects the nature of our assessment of inequality and injustice. Several authors (such as Weale 1978, Rae 1981, Fishkin 1983, Walzer 1983) have powerfully pointed towards plural conceptions of equality. This is indeed a valuable point to note. On the other hand, the source of the plurality of equality often does not lie in the nature of equality itself, but in the concept of the advantage of a person. If advantages are viewed differently, then so must be the assessment of equality. The same plurality would apply to other 'derivative' concepts that rely – exclusively or inclusively – on the notion of advantage. Indeed, in this respect the concept of 'efficiency' is as much open to plural interpretations as is equality, since the non-existence of another feasible state more advantageous for all is throughly dependent on the chosen concept of advantage. When, for example, advantage is equated with utility, efficiency coincides with Pareto optimality. As the notion of advantage is altered, so is the content of efficiency, just as much as the content of equality is also similarly altered. The notion of advantage need not, of course, take a scalar form, and may be seen as a vector or as an n-tuple, and it may include some 'constitutive plurality' as well as competitively plural interpretations. These issues are discussed in Sen (1980, 1985a, 1985b).

[19] On Bentham's discussion of moral and natural rights, see Harrison (1983, Chapter IV). Marx (1843) was no less dismissive than Bentham of 'the so-called rights of man' but at the same time emphasized the importance of the perspective of positive freedom in general (Marx 1844, 1875, Marx and Engels 1845–6). Part of the contrast lies in Marx's emphasis on the role of the political state in creating and supporting what are often seen as 'fundamental human rights'. On the other hand, Marx's own moral philosophy strongly incorporated what has been called an 'ethics of freedom' (Brenkert 1983). For different

however, been so easy to dispose of, and despite the long dominance of utilitarianism in ethics, they have recently been powerfully revived again, in different ways, by such writers as Kanger (1957, 1985), Rawls (1971), Nozick (1974), Dworkin (1978), Mackie (1978), among others.[20]

In economics the concept of rights is often invoked, and indeed the basic economic concepts of endowment, exchange, contract, etc., all involve various types of rights. However, under the utilitarian tradition, these rights were viewed as entirely instrumental to achieving other goods, in particular utilities. No intrinsic importance is attached to the existence or fulfilment of rights, and they have been judged by their ability to achieve good consequences, among which the fulfilment of rights have not figured.

This particular tradition has been carried into the *post*-utilitarian phase of welfare economics, concentrating on Pareto optimality and efficiency. This is not surprising since the rejection of attaching intrinsic importance to rights comes from welfarism in general rather than from utilitarianism *per se* (i.e. the specific feature of sum-ranking is not particularly crucial in the rejection of rights-based ethical accounting). It is fair to say that the view that rights cannot be intrinsically important is fairly ingrained in the economic tradition now established, and this is partly due to the influence of utilitarianism (and specifically of welfarism, as a part of that package), but also due to the lack of interest

---

aspects of Marx's complex approach to rights and freedoms, see Bose (1975), Cohen (1978), Buchanan (1982), Roemer (1982), Lukes (1985), Elster (1986).

[20] Waldron (1984) provides a useful collection of papers on the subject, along with an illuminating introduction. See also Feinberg (1980) and Gauthier (1986). On related matters see Atkinson (1975, 1983), Archibald and Donaldson (1979), Pettit (1980), Dasgupta (1982b, 1986) and Wiggins (1985).

that welfare economics has had in any kind of complex ethical theory.

Concentration on what was called in the first lecture the 'engineering' aspect of economics has tended to go hand in hand with sticking to a very narrow view of ethics. It is arguable that the utilitarian criterion, and also that of Pareto efficiency, have appealed particularly because they have not especially taxed the ethical imagination of the conventional economist.[21] While a questioning economist like John Hicks (1959) may argue that the classical backing for 'economic freedom' went deeper than justifying it on grounds of 'economic efficiency', which provided 'no more than a secondary support' to freedom, and while he is certainly cogent in questioning the justification for our 'forgetting, as completely as most of us have done, the other side of the argument' (p. 138), such protests have been rather rarely made, and even more rarely followed up.[22] It cannot be doubted that the issue of

---

[21] Indeed, mainstream economics has tended to ignore even the more complex and refined versions of utilitarianism itself, e.g. those involving 'indirect relations' (see, for example, Sidgwick 1874, Hare 1981, Hammond 1982, Harsanyi 1982, Mirrlees 1982, Raz 1986), concentrating instead on the simpler – more 'direct' – versions.

[22] The perspective of freedom and rights has, however, received attention from theorists influenced by libertarian views, e.g. Hayek (1960), Nozick (1974), Friedman and Friedman (1980), and Buchanan (1985, 1986); see also Buchanan and Tullock (1962), Usher (1981), Brittan (1983), Sugden (1985). Even though the libertarian approach to freedom and rights is, I believe, arbitrarily limited (as I have argued in Sen 1983a, 1985c), there cannot be any question that libertarian writings and related contributions have served as a major creative influence in economics and as an important challenge to the utilitarian orthodoxy. Another group involved in reviving interest in the role of rights and freedom have been contributors to social choice theory, e.g. Sen (1970a, 1970c, 1976c, 1983a), Ng (1971), Batra and Pattanaik

rights and freedom places an important question mark on the general approach of welfarism (including *inter alia* utilitarianism and Pareto optimality).[23] This question will indeed be pursued in some detail in the third lecture.

Self-interest and Welfare Economics

In this lecture I have been concentrating so far on the impoverishment of welfare economics as a result of the distance that has grown between ethics and economics, and particularly on the inadequacy of the evaluative criteria used in economics, especially modern welfare economics. But I began this lecture by referring to the directional asymmetry that has been arbitrarily imposed between

---

(1972), Peacock and Rowley (1972), Nozick (1973, 1974), Bernholz (1974, 1980), Gibbard (1974), Blau (1975), Fine (1975b), Seidl (1975), Campbell (1976), Farrell (1976), Kelly (1976a, 1976b, 1978), Aldrich (1977), Breyer (1977), Perelli-Minetti (1977), Ferejohn (1978), Karni (1978), Stevens and Foster (1978), Suzumura (1978, 1980, 1983), Austen-Smith (1979, 1982), Mueller (1979), Barnes (1980), Breyer and Gardner (1980), Breyer and Gigliotti (1980), Fountain (1980), Gardner (1980), Green (1980), McLean (1980), Weale (1980), Gaertner and Krüger (1981, 1983), Gärdenfors (1981), Hammond (1981, 1982, 1985), Schwartz (1981, 1986), Sugden (1981, 1985), Levi (1982, 1985), Wriglesworth (1982, 1985), Chapman (1983), Krüger and Gaertner (1983), Basu (1984), Gaertner (1985, 1986), Kelsey (1985), Schotter (1985), Barry (1986), Elster (1986), Hylland (1986), Mackie (1986), Webster (1986). Wriglesworth (1985) has provided an illuminating guide to the literature, in addition to making his own contributions.

[23] I have examined this aspect of the problem in Sen (1970a, 1979a,b). For defences of welfarism, see Harsanyi (1976), Hare (1981), Ng (1981), Mirrlees (1982). Arguments and counter-arguments can be found in Smart and Williams (1973), and Sen and Williams (1982). See also Riley (1986) and Roemer (1986a, 1986b).

predictive economics and welfare economics, with the former being taken into account in the latter, but without any influence coming from the opposite direction. If, however, the actual behaviour of human beings is affected by ethical considerations (and influencing human conduct is after all, a central aspect of ethics), then clearly welfare–economic considerations must be allowed to have some impact on actual behaviour and must therefore be relevant for predictive economics also. Indeed it would be rather absurd to devote much attention to the subject of ethics if it were really the case that ethical considerations would never affect people's actual behaviour.

The sense of invulnerability from ethics that predictive economics seems to enjoy arises partly from the alleged force of the hypothesis that human behaviour, at least in economic matters, can be well approximated by self-interest maximization. A substantial part of the first lecture was devoted to questioning this behavioural assumption. The time has now come to link up that discussion regarding actual behaviour (and the underlying concept of rationality used as an intermediary) and the present discussion about the ethical foundations of welfare economics. It is easy to see that if welfare economic considerations affect actual behaviour, then the nature of acceptable welfare economics must be rather important for description, explanation and prediction of economic occurrences.

Indeed, if economic efficiency (in the sense of Pareto optimality) were the only criterion for economic judgement, and if the various conditions (such as no externality) imposed by the so-called 'Fundamental Theorem of Welfare Economics' were to hold, then there would be in general no welfare–economic argument for anyone to behave in a way other than that required for self-interest maximization. Such behaviour on the part of all will indeed produce Pareto optimality, and the attempt on the part of anyone to depart from self-interest maximization would, if it would do anything, only threaten the achievement of 'economic efficiency', i.e. Pareto optimality. Therefore, if welfare economics is in fact put in this extremely narrow box, and if the structural assumptions were to hold (including ruling out non-market interdependences), then there would indeed be no welfare–economic case against self-interested behaviour. Thus, given the structural assumptions, the one-sided format of the relation between predictive and welfare economics, which can be seen in the dominant economic tradition, is entirely sustainable as long as welfare economics is confined to the narrow box proclaiming the adequacy of Pareto optimality. As and when that narrow box is busted by bringing in broader ethical considerations, the sustainability of the one-sided relationship must also disappear.

In the next stage of the examination, it may be asked what would be the consequence of taking a more demanding welfarist criterion, such as utilitarianism. This would certainly be adequate for rejecting the optimality of self-interested behaviour in many circumstances. Indeed, Francis Edgeworth (1881) saw the conflict of principles in the determination of individual behaviour as one between 'egoism' on the one hand, and 'utilitarianism' on the other. It is, of course, true that the utilitarian optimum must be *inter alia* Pareto optimal, and also true that – under the circumstances demanded by the so-called 'fundamental theorem' – any departure from self-interested behaviour may well threaten the achievement of Pareto optimality. But it is not true that any movement from a Pareto optimal state to a non-Pareto optimal one must reduce the aggregate utility. Indeed frequently that will not be the case.

However, as was discussed earlier, the 'Fundamental Theorem of Welfare Economics' would yield a justification of self-interested behaviour on the part of each *if* the initial distribution of endowments is appropriate for the chosen welfarist objective. The overall scheme admitted of circumstances in which acting entirely according to self-interest *could* be ethically fully justified. Then, once again, welfare–economic considerations would not reject self-interested behaviour, and consequently predictive economic analysis could be free from any 'infection' from welfare economics. The practical significance of this part of the 'fundamental theorem' may well be very limited, for reasons that were discussed earlier, involving informational, economic and political difficulties. But at the theoretical level this structure of assumptions made it again possible to see human beings as exclusively pursuing self-interest, without fear of some contrary welfare–economic advice, provided the appropriate conditions could be assumed.

At this stage of the analysis, we have moved from the narrowest box to broader ones, without precipitating any *necessary* rejection of self-interested behaviour on welfare–economic grounds (the 'initial conditions' bearing a lot of the weight in this reconciliation). But at all these stages, welfarism is playing an important part in achieving this feature. So long as the evaluative criterion is welfarist, whether it is simply Pareto optimality, or some other more complex welfarist criterion (such as utilitarianism), the necessity of having welfare–economic departures from self-interest maximization in actual behaviour is conditionally eliminated.

In the next stage, if welfarism itself is rejected, then the 'fundamental theorem' cannot any longer guarantee this conditional independence of actual behaviour from the relevance of welfare–economic considerations. The various departures from welfarism discussed earlier in this lecture may all provide grounds for rejecting self-interested behaviour.

This is most obviously so when importance is attached to the 'agency aspect' of a person. Indeed, the person himself or herself may have reasons for pursuing goals *other than* personal well-being or individual self-interest. Respect for the agency aspect of *others* can also lead to similar departures. Self-interested behaviour can scarcely suffice when agency is important on its own (and is not simply reducible to the pursuit of self-interest).

Another type of problem arises from adopting a notion of well-being that differs from utility, since the 'fundamental theorem' is not easily translatable into other ways of judging individual well-being. A view of well-being not primarily based on preference, but on some 'objective' circumstances (e.g. a person's functioning achievements)[24] may also undermine the simplicity of the picture of self-interested choice implicit in the behavioural assumptions underlying the 'fundamental theorem'. While choice may well diverge from preference, it can diverge much more easily from these other, non-preference-based notions of well-being.

---

[24] See, for instance, Sen (1970a, 1985a), Scanlon (1975), Broome (1978), Schwartz (1982), Nussbaum (1986c). See also the development literature dealing with criteria of 'objective' achievements such as fulfilling 'basic needs' (see for example Sen 1973c, Adelman 1975, Fishlow 1978, Grant 1978, Streeten and Burki 1978, Morris 1979, Chichilnisky 1980, Streeten 1981a, 1981b, Dasgupta 1982b, Anand 1983, Bardhan 1984, Stewart 1985). The case for going beyond the metric of individual preferences and for attaching special value to the fulfilment of 'merit wants' was presented by Musgrave (1959). Concentrating on minimal conditions of life goes back to Pigou's (1952) own analysis, though he related the value of these achievements ultimately to utility. The real issue is not the relevance of basic needs fulfilment, but the *foundation* of that concern. I have discussed this question in Sen (1985a, 1985b).

Rights and Freedom

The inadequacy of self-interested behaviour can also be serious in ethical approaches that emphasize rights and freedoms. This fact might not be quite obvious. Some theories of rights, e.g. that of Nozick (1974), assert the right of a person to pursue anything he likes provided he does not violate the deontological constraints that restrain him from interfering in the legitimate activities of another. The person is free to pursue self-interest (subject to those constraints) without let or hindrance. It must, however, be recognized that the *existence* of these rights does not indicate that it would be ethically appropriate to *exercise* them through self-interested behaviour. The existence of such a right restrains others from stopping this person if he *were* to pursue self-interest maximization, but that is not a reason for actually pursuing self-interest. In fact, a theory of rights like that of Nozick can be combined even with asserting the moral appropriateness on the part of each person in the society to think how he might help others. If the ethical case for going beyond self-interested behaviour is to be rejected, this could not, thus, be on grounds of the priority of these rights.

This is so even when the rights are conceived of in so-called 'negative' terms (e.g. rejecting interference, rather than giving a positive right to be helped by others). Indeed, *valuing* 'negative freedom' – as opposed to merely obeying the corresponding constraints – may have implications in favour of conduct in positive defence of such freedom of others, e.g. a duty to help others when they are threatened with violation of negative rights.[25] And, of course, it is

---

[25] The case for 'a positive concept of negative freedom' is discussed in

clear that emphasizing *positive* freedom (i.e. a person being actually able to do this or be that), and the duty to help others in that respect as well, could strengthen the relevance of ethical considerations in the determination of actual behaviour (see Sen 1980, 1985c).[26] Moral acceptance of rights (especially rights that are valued and supported, and not just respected in the form of constraints) may call for systematic departures from self-interested behaviour. Even a partial and limited move in that direction in actual conduct can shake the behavioural foundations of standard economic theory.[27]

The impoverishment of economics related to its distancing from ethics affects both *welfare economics* (narrowing its reach and relevance) and *predictive economics* (weakening its behavioural foundations). In the third and final lecture I shall go further into the demands of systematic ethical evaluation, and the role of consequences, freedom and rights in this evaluation. The bearing of such broader ethical considerations on actual behaviour, and thus on predictive economics, will also have to be examined.

Sen (1981b, 1982b). See also Usher (1981), Dasgupta (1982b, 1986), Hammond (1982), Frey (1983), Helm (1986), and Raz (1986).

[26] See also Kanger (1957, 1972), Kanger and Kanger (1966), Rawls (1971), Lindahl (1977), Dworkin (1978), Haksar (1979), Feinberg (1980), James (1982), Wiggins (1985), Goodin (1985), Gauthier (1986), O'Neill (1986), Raz (1986).

[27] These questions are further pursued in the third lecture.

3 Freedom and Consequences

In the last lecture I discussed how the conceptualization of personal achievement and advantage in welfare economics has been deeply influenced by the utilitarian view of the person and how this influence continues to be important even in the post-utilitarian phase of welfare economics. The utilitarian conception, it was argued, is narrow and inadequate, and it has been further impoverished in modern welfare economics by the imposition of some additional limitations, especially the eschewing of inter-personal comparisons of utility. That additional impoverishment can be countered by returning to a more full-blooded utilitarian conception. But that will do nothing to remove the indigent nature of the basic utilitarian view of the person.

Well-being, Agency and Freedom

In the last lecture, three distinct limitations of the utilitarian conception were identified, and they are essentially independent of each other. In trying to go beyond, particular attention has to be paid to the nature of these limitations and how they can be overcome.

First, we have to distinguish between the 'well-being aspect' and the 'agency aspect' of a person. The former covers the person's achievements and opportunities in the context of his or her personal advantage, whereas the latter goes further and examines achievements and opportunities in terms of other objectives and values as well, possibly going well beyond the pursuit of one's own well-being. Both these aspects command attention, but do so in distinct ways and for different reasons. The 'well-being aspect' is particularly important in assessing issues of distributive justice (including diagnosing economic injustice) and in evaluating the nature of the 'deal' that the person has in terms of personal advantage. The 'agency aspect' takes a wider view of the person, including valuing the various things he or she would want to see happen, and the ability to form such objectives and to have them realized.[1]

While both well-being and agency are active concepts since both involve various functionings (on which see Sen 1985a,b), and the distinction between these two aspects does not correspond to that between a 'patient' and an 'agent', the agency aspect pays more complete attention to the person as a *doer*. The distinction does not, of course, entail that a person's agency is independent of his or her well-being. As was discussed in Lecture 2, it is natural to expect that no substantial variation in one can be achieved without some variation in the other. But they are nevertheless not identical, nor so closely linked that one can be seen as a mere transformation of the other. The utilitarian treatment of the person suffers from a failure to distinguish between these different aspects, and from trying to motivate normative evaluation on the basis of the well-being aspect alone.

Second, the utilitarian conception provides a defective

---

[1] The necessity of considering both these aspects for normative evaluation was discussed in my Dewey Lectures (Sen 1985a, pp. 185–7, 203–8).

(and systematically biased) view of well-being, and the limitations of the different interpretations of utility (e.g. happiness, desire-fulfilment) were analysed in that context. While being happy is a momentous achievement, it is not the only achievement that matters to one's well-being (on this, see Rawls 1971). Also, while desire is often a good indicator of the valuable nature of what is desired, the metric of desire can be a very inadequate reflection of value – indeed even of what the person himself or herself actually values, not to mention what he or she would value on serious and courageous reflection, freed from the limitations imposed by unfavourable circumstances. This limitation is particularly serious in the context of interpersonal comparisons of well-being.

Third, a person's freedom can be seen as being valuable in addition to his or her achievements. A person's options and opportunities can be seen as counting in a normative evaluation, in addition to what the person ends up achieving or securing. Freedom may be valued not merely because it assists achievement, but also because of its own importance, going beyond the value of the state of existence actually achieved. If, for example, all the alternatives other than the one actually chosen were to be eliminated, this need not affect achievement (since the chosen alternative can be still chosen), but the person clearly has less freedom, and this may be seen as a loss of some importance.[2]

---

[2] An alternative way of seeing freedom is through characterizing 'functionings' in a 'refined' way (see Sen 1985a, pp. 200–2), taking note of the alternatives that were available. For example, choosing x when y is available may be seen as different from choosing x when y is not available. The language commonly used sometimes does, in fact, take a 'refined' form, e.g. 'fasting' is not just starving, but doing so despite having the option not to starve. Fasting may well be assessed

The perspective of freedom can be applied to the 'well-being aspect' as well as to the 'agency aspect'. There are, therefore, *four* distinct categories of relevant information regarding a person, involving 'well-being achievement', 'well-being freedom', 'agency achievement', and 'agency freedom'.[3] In the standard format of mainstream welfare economics, this plurality is reduced to a single category by the dual procedure of

1 seeing freedom as being *only instrumentally* valuable (so that ultimately only achievement counts);
2 assuming that everyone's agency is *exclusively* geared to the pursuit of self-interest (so that agency has no separate role either).

I have already discussed (in Lecture 2) why that arbitrarily limited informational structure is inadequate.

Plurality and Evaluation

The multiplicity of categories of ethically relevant information has been seen as a problem in some traditions.[4] Indeed, in the utilitarian approach all the diverse goods are reduced into a homogeneous descriptive magnitude (as utility is supposed to be), and then the ethical evaluation simply takes the form of a monotonic transformation of that magnitude. Of course, in so far as the ethical evaluation is supposed to take ultimately the form of a

---

differently from other types of starving precisely because of the 'choice' element implicit in the 'refined' description.
[3] I have tried to discuss the distinct roles of these four categories in my Dewey Lectures (Sen 1985a).
[4] The main issues have been identified and examined by Steiner (1983).

complete and transitive ordering, possibly with a numerical representation, there might be, I suppose, nothing *formally* odd in conceptualizing goodness as a homogeneous ethical value. I shall presently argue that that view itself – seeing goodness in terms of a necessarily complete and transitive ordering – is far too restrictive and deficient, but it is worth emphasizing here that the insistence on descriptive homogeneity of the *object* of value in the form of some quantity of utility is an additional – and far more restrictive – requirement. Not only is there a unified and complete view of ethical goodness (weighing the different objects of value vis-a-vis each other), but even the objects of value must be all of the *same* type (singular and homogeneous) in this 'monist' conception.

The multiplicity of ethically valuable considerations involved in our framework which attaches importance both to well-being and agency, and sees each in terms of achievement and freedom, would of course be embarrassing for a 'monist' methodology, which insists on descriptive homogeneity of what is to be valued. However, the arbitrarily restrictive nature of that 'monist' approach does little to make that criterion forceful, and I shall not dwell here further on the reasons for not being deterred by 'monist' objections (I have discussed this question elsewhere, Sen 1985a).

The issue of pluralism and diversity of goods, and the implications that they have on rational ethics, will certainly need attention, if only because these meta-ethical problems are both rather unclear and obviously quite important for welfare economics. I am not dismissing the importance of these general questions, and indeed I shall try to address them later on in this lecture. What is being asserted here is a refusal to see the problem in terms of an *a priori* need for descriptive homogeneity of what is to be valued. This arbitrary requirement of descriptive homogeneity of the objects of value has to be clearly distinguished from the question as to whether ethical evaluation must lead to a complete and consistent order.[5] The important – and entirely non-arbitrary – problem of ordering diverse bundles of goods certainly remains, and will have to be addressed when dealing with the major question of ethical conflicts. But the issue of ethical ordering must not be confused with that of descriptive homogeneity.[6]

It should also be added that the nature of the plurality may, in fact, be much more extensive in the approach under discussion here than the fourfold classification of the categories of moral information may suggest. This is because there are diversities *within* each of these categories. For example, 'well-being achievement' will require that note be taken of the *various* important things a person

---

[5] The issue of 'commensurability', much discussed in ethics, seems to involve both these different aspects – that of descriptive homogeneity of goods, and that of consistent and complete overall ordering. Both these issues have figured in ethical discussions over a long time, including in classical Greek philosophy and literature (on this see Nussbaum 1984, 1985, 1986a). See also Williams (1973b, 1981), Berlin (1978), Nagel (1979), Marcus (1980), Searle (1980), Hampshire (1982), Taylor (1982), Foot (1983), Steiner (1983), Levi (1986a).

[6] Ordering diverse bundles of good objects is, of course, a standard part of economics (see Deaton and Muellbauer 1980). For example, commodity bundles differ in the composition of good characteristics and may be taken to be fully ordered on the many-dimensional space of characteristics (see Gorman, 1956, 1976; Lancaster 1966, 1971). While in the traditional approach the ordering is supposed to reflect the amounts of a homogeneous object, namely, satisfaction, no such requirement is imposed in more modern versions of consumer theory, in which 'utility' is simply the real-valued representation of an ordering (specifically, the one revealed by choice). The ordering of diverse bundles of good characteristics may or may not be problematic in a particular case, but certainly an ordering does not require descriptive homogeneity.

succeeds in doing or being. These 'functionings' may cover a diverse range of achievements, varying from being free from under-nourishment and avoidable morbidity to achieving self-respect and creative fulfilment.[7] In fact, it is in this list that the functioning of 'being happy', which some utilitarians see as the basis of *all* valuation, can – not unreasonably – *inter alia* figure.

This internal diversity is carried into the evaluation of 'well-being *freedom*' as well, and in addition there is diversity there arising from the different ways in which a *set* could be evaluated even when the *elements* of the set all have clearly specified values – a problem I have discussed elsewhere (Sen 1985b). There are corresponding diversities within 'agency achievement' and 'agency freedom'.

Furthermore, as we move from the achievements and freedom of a person to that of a set of many persons – inescapably involved in most economic judgements and ethical evaluations – the nature of the plurality is further enhanced. If, in fact, plurality were regarded as an embarrassment in itself, this would have been a totally hopeless way to proceed. There is, however, nothing particularly embarrassing in a plural framework, and the insistence on 'monist' frameworks cannot escape being arbitrarily exclusive.

As it happens, the analytical frameworks developed by social choice theory have addressed the problem of plural evaluation in many different contexts, including normative assessment (see Sen 1970a, 1986c). Indeed that entire literature, pioneered by Arrow (1951a), takes such plurality for

---

[7] See Sen (1980, 1985a,b). The approach of functionings and capabilities developed in these works can be seen as having something in common with Aristotle's analysis of functions (see *Politics*, Book III). For an examination of the Aristotelian approach, and its relation to contemporary discussions on well-being, see Nussbaum (1986c).

granted. Furthermore, since in some economic-theoretical exercises, the term utility is often used interchangeably with *valuation*, the analytical problems studied *within* the structure of 'utility functions' offer some substantial insights about the nature of plural evaluation as well. The problems of completeness and consistency in these various contexts have received a good deal of attention, and the formal literature of social choice theory in particular is full of various 'impossibility theorems' as well as positive possibility results and constructive characterization theorems closely related to pluralities.

What has to be asked in this context is the acceptability and adequacy of the regularity conditions that have been imposed in the formulation of aggregate assessment, related to particular notions of 'rational evaluation'.

Incompleteness and Overcompleteness

When there are several objects of value, one alternative course of action may be more valued in one respect but less so in another. There are three different ways of dealing with this problem. The first is to examine the appropriate 'trade-offs' and to decide whether *on balance* one alternative combination of objects is superior to another.[8] This approach asks that the conflicts be 'resolved' *before* decisions are taken. This leaves open the question as to what is to be done if the conflicts are unresolved.

---

[8] Such balancing may, however, involve 'tragic choices', calling for appropriate recognition of the nature of sacrifices that would be involved (see the illuminating account of Calabresi and Bobbitt 1978). Isaac Levi (1986a) has recently provided a far-reaching investigation of the related problem of deciding on action in 'hard choices' when some conflicts have not been balanced into resolved judgements.

In contrast with the 'balanced complete ordering' the second approach may leave two alternatives unordered. This approach does not demand a *complete* ordering in each case, and permits incompleteness in the partial order emerging from plural evaluation (on this, see Sen 1970a, 1985a). When there is a congruence of the different parts of the plural evaluation, a clear overall ranking can, of course, be reached on the basis of 'dominance reasoning', i.e. 'x is better than y in all respects'. The partial ordering ultimately arrived at will *include* the dominance relation but may of course go much further.

Both the approaches of 'balanced complete ordering' and 'partial orders' insist on simple consistency. The third approach goes against that, and faced with an irreducible conflict of compelling principles, it may admit both the superiority of one alternative over the other and the converse. It is fair to say that this approach – admitting 'inconsistent' judgements – finds little favour among economists, and indeed most philosophers. It may, in fact, appear straightforwardly bizarre in terms of the standard requirements of internal consistency.

To recognize such 'inconsistency' does not, however, demolish the third approach, since both the *feasibility* and the *necessity* of such 'consistency' also require justification (on this see Sen 1967b, 1984c). This last possibility can result from accepting the compelling nature of two potentially conflicting principles of overall judgement with an overlapping domain. These 'overcomplete judgements' relate to issues discussed a great deal in classical literature and philosophy. Whatever view one may take of, say, Agamemnon's dilemma, it can scarcely be solved by simply demanding that Agamemnon should lick his preference ordering to shape before he gets going.[9]

---

[9] See Bernard Williams (1965, 1973b, 1981) and Martha Nussbaum

In discussing these different approaches, it is, I believe, important to distinguish between the requirements of institutional public policy, on the one hand, and those of personal decisions, on the other. In the context of institutional public policy, the case for following the first approach – that of 'balanced complete ordering' – is indeed strong, and it is not difficult to sympathize with the need for consistent and complete social welfare functions in that context, or with the need for complete social choice functions, specifying non-empty choice sets for all non-empty sets of alternatives to choose from (see Fishburn 1973 on the last). This is not only because an institution-based public decision must, at some stage, require unambiguous instruction, but also because whatever value there might be in acknowledging the 'richness' of inconsistency arising from conflicts of principles, is typically personal to the individual involved in the conflict.

Indeed, needs of policy do require that something or other *must* be ultimately done; if only nothing, which is one such something. However, it does not follow – and this is the important point to get across – that there must be *adequate reason* for choosing one course rather than another. Incompleteness or overcompleteness in overall judgements might well be a damned nuisance for decisions, but the *need* for a decision does not, on its own, *resolve* the conflict. This implies that sometimes even institutional public decisions may have to be taken on the basis of partial justification.

There is, I believe, no departure from rational choice in this acceptance. For example, Buridan's ass, which died of

---

(1985, 1986a). On related issues, see also Lemmon (1962), Walzer (1973), Elster (1979, 1983), Nagel (1979), Marcus (1980), Searle (1980), Hare (1982), Finnis (1983), Slote (1983, 1986), Steiner (1983), Levi (1986a), and Steedman and Krause (1986).

hunger being unable to decide which of the two haystacks in front of it happened to be superior, could have rationally chosen either of the haystacks, since it had good reason for choosing *either* rather than starving to death. But it had not enough reason to choose one haystack *rather than* the other, and choosing either of them, would have been thus only partially justified. Rational public decisions have to come to terms with such partially justified choices.[10]

Conflicts and Impasse

When it comes to *personal* judgements and decisions, the recognition of diversity of goods with unclear 'trade-offs', and the impossibility – if that is the case – of arriving at a complete ordering may have some psychological and ethical relevance. Of course, here too the requirements of decision will call for either balancing, or some arbitrary resolution of an impasse, but that is not the only thing that is important in human reflection and volition. For example, even if some hard-headed piece of unresponsive ruthlessness turns out to be optimally conducive to good economic consequences, taking into account indirect effects, it is still not absurd to think that there is something of serious

---

[10] I have discussed the usefulness and adequacy of the approach of 'partial ordering' in Sen (1970a,b, 1985a,b). It should also be noted here that a complete ordering may not be needed for the existence of a 'best' element in a given set. Some inconsistency and incompleteness may be admissible without embarrassing optimal choice. On the analytical issues involved, see Sen (1970a, 1971, 1982a, 1984c, 1986c), Fishburn (1973), Plott (1976), Schwartz (1976, 1986), Kelly (1978), Pattanaik (1978), Moulin (1983), Suzumura (1983), Peleg (1984), Aizerman (1985). The really difficult questions arise when there is no 'best' element in the set from which we have to choose (due to incompleteness, overcompleteness, or intransitivity). On this and related matters, see Sen (1984c), and Levi (1986a).

disvalue in being unable to be coolly ruthless and unresponsive to requests for help.

The value of these dilemmas, and of their psychological correlates in the form of pause, hesitation, grief, etc.,[11] is obviusly greater for many cultural and social activities than it may be for economic decisions. But these conflicts and the consequent impasse cannot be altogether irrelevant to economics either, since they may influence the behaviour of human beings whose actions economics tries to study.

Recent empirical studies of behaviour under uncertainty has brought out what has appeared to be systematic inconsistencies in the evaluation of risk and in the comparative assessment of alternative decisions.[12] Many of these results have been interpreted, perhaps with some justice, as simply 'mistakes' in perception or reasoning. Even if that view is fully accepted, the prevalence of such behaviour indicates the case for making room for departures from the usual requirements of 'rationality' in understanding actual behaviour. But it is also arguable that some of these so-called 'mistakes', in fact, only reflect a different view of the decision problem, in contrast with that formalized in the standard literature.[13]

The scope for broadening our understanding of decision

---

[11] On this see Williams (1985) and Nussbaum (1986a).

[12] See particularly Keeney and Raiffa (1976), Kahneman, Slovik and Tversky (1982). Also Allais (1953), Allais and Hagen (1979), Davidson, Suppes and Siegel (1957), MacCrimmon (1968), Kahneman and Tversky (1979), and Arrow (1982, 1983). See also Levi (1974, 1982, 1986a, 1986b), Machina (1981), Bell (1982), Loomes and Sugden (1982), McClennen (1983), Schelling (1984), Davidson (1985b), Sen (1985e), on various related issues. Also the essays presented in Stigum and Wenstop (1983), and Daboni, Montesano and Lines (1986).

[13] I have argued in that direction in Sen (1984c, 1985d, 1985e). See also Machina (1981), Broome (1984), Hammond (1986).

problems in the context of ethical arguments and welfare–economic assessment is considerable. In fact, the model of 'balanced complete ordering' may be unrealistic and deeply deceptive for description and prediction of behaviour, in addition to being possibly unreasonable in substantive ethics. Obviously, there is no great case for inventing deeply divisive dilemmas when none exists, but when they do exist – as they seem to often enough – recognizing the nature of these dilemmas may add not only to the understanding and assessment of economic phenomena, they may also help in economic prediction.

Problems of this kind can be particularly important in labour relations (involving joining strikes or helping to break them), wage negotiations (involving collective industrial action or threat thereof), industrial efficiency and productivity (involving cooperation and conflict within the factory), and a number of other contexts which are by no means unimportant to the working of an economy (see Sen 1984a). For example, in examining the complex process of the coal-miners' strike that took place in Britain during 1984–5, with varying proportions of striking and strike-breaking miners, the ethical complexity and pragmatic demands faced by the miners have to be adequately understood. While the game-theoretic aspects of the problem can be formalized up to a point within the structure of traditional models of narrow rationality, the severe restrictions imposed by that model are quite limiting.

Rights and Consequences

The richness of ethical considerations that might be relevant to both welfare economics and predictive economics is, thus, much greater than what has been traditionally accommodated or proposed in these fields. The restrictions imposed by both welfarism and consequentialism as well as by the demands of narrowly-conceived rational decisions have made many different types of relevant considerations inadmissible in economic evaluation or behavioural prediction. I have tried to argue that this calls for a remedial expansion of the set of variables and influences that find room in economic analysis.

While this discussion has been rather critical of economics as it stands, it is not my intention to suggest that these problems have been very satisfactorily dealt with in the existing ethical literature, so that all that would need to be done would be to incorporate the lessons from that literature into economics, by getting it closer to ethics. This, alas, is not the case. In fact, it is arguable that some of these ethical considerations can be helpfully analysed further by using various approaches and procedures utilized in economics itself.

The point can be illustrated in terms of the idea of moral rights and freedom. It must, of course, be admitted straightaway that moral rights or freedom are not, in fact, concepts for which modern economics has much time. In fact, in economic analysis rights are seen typically as purely legal entities with instrumental use rather than any intrinsic value. I have already discussed these neglects. However, it is arguable that an adequate formulation of rights and of freedom can make substantial use of consequential reasoning of the type standardly used in economics.

In the revival of rights-based ethics in recent decades, rights have often been seen in deontological terms, taking the form of constraints that others simply must obey. Robert Nozick's (1974) elegant system of a rights-based moral structure is a case in point. It is arguable that this type of deontological structure may not be particularly suitable for focusing on complex problems of pervasive interdependence involved in social morality (including normative economics). For example, if there is imperfect compliance, and some do not actually obey the relevant constraints (this may indeed by a very common situation), should others not try to prevent these violations? But such moral requirements, if present, would not themselves take the form of constraints, but of obligations to do something positive, to wit, to try to stop the violators.

If person A is violating in a serious way some right of B, e.g. beating him up badly, does person C have a duty to help prevent this?[14] Further, would C be justified in doing some minor violation of some other right of person D to help prevent the more important violation of B's rights by strong-armed A? Could C, for example, take without permission – let us say by force – a car belonging to D who

---

[14] Accepting such a duty may, of course, also be based on utilitarian reasoning since B's utility – and not merely his rights – suffers in the hands of A. The purpose of this example is to compare right-based reasoning of different types, without comparing them respectively with utilitarian argumentation. However, if the purpose is to illustrate the advantage of consequential, right-based reasoning not merely over non-consequential, deontological formulations of rights, but also over utilitarianism, the example could be so extended as to give C no utilitarian reason to intervene. This can be easily done for 'act utilitarianism' by making the total utility gain of the aggressor (or more plausibility, *many* aggressors) greater than the utility loss of victim B. Indeed, the example can be so constructed that even equity-conscious welfarists (and not merely utilitarians who maximize just the utility *sum*) would have no reason to recommend C's intervention (e.g. victim B may be very well off and may remain better off than the lumpen attackers even with the assault). Indirect utilitarian and related welfarist positions require some further consideration, which too can be provided without compromising the illustrative purpose of this type of example, i.e. the special advantages of incorporating right fulfilments and violations in a consequential framework. These issues have been more fully discussed, with illustrations, in Sen (1982b, 1983c).

will not lend it to C, to rush to the spot to rescue B from being beaten up by A. If rights only take the form of constraints ('Do not violate the rights of others'), and the constraints are as they are specified in, say, Nozick's system, then C clearly must not try to help B in this way, since C is:

1 under no obligation to help B,
2 he is under an obligation *not* to violate D's rights.

The Nozickian entitlement system of rights offers unplausible answers to these and many related questions, but these questions are inescapably important if rights are indeed to be taken seriously and supported.

I have tried to argue elsewhere (Sen 1982b, 1985c) that this type of 'general interdependence' calls for internalization of external accounting in a way that is better dealt with by incorporating the value of right fulfilment and the disvalue of right violation in the assessment of resulting states of affairs.[15] The framework of consequential reasoning and pursuit of interdependences extensively developed in economics in many different contexts (including that of general equilibrium analysis, discussed in Lecture 2) provide many insights into pursuing the inescapable problems of interdependence involved in valuing rights in a society.

---

[15] Steiner (1986) has critically examined my proposal and made important suggestions. In the seminar (in February 1986, at Louvain-la-Neuve) in which Steiner's paper was presented, there were other interesting examinations of the approach I have tried to pursue (particularly from Jos de Beus). I am most grateful to the organizers of the seminar (Leo Apostel and Philippe Van Parijs) and to the participants.

Consequential Assessment and Deontology

This type of treatment of rights tends to meet with some resistance, especially since the revival of rights-based reasoning has frequently come from philosophical positions suspicious of consequentialist reasoning (e.g. Rawls 1971, Nozick 1974, Dworkin 1978, Ackerman 1980). The suspicion is aroused that rejecting the view of rights as unrelaxable deontological constraints might have the effect of throwing the baby out with the bathwater. The intrinsic importance of rights may get compromised by consequential counterarguments, and such compromises may be ethically indefensible, since they may make rights flimsy and unduly contingent.

It is understandable that such doubts might plausibly arise. However, the fears are essentially misplaced. First, they arise to some extent from the tradition of combining consequentialism with *welfarism*, whereby not only are actions, etc., judged by the goodness of states of affairs, but the goodness of states of affairs, in its turn, is judged entirely by utility consequences. The fact that utilitarianism incorporates both consequentialism and welfarism has often made it difficult to separate out the two elements. But they are of course distinct and essentially independent elements.[16]

Indeed, if rights violations are treated as bad things and rights fulfilments as good things, welfarism must be compromised, since welfarism requires that nothing else be intrinsically valued other than utilities. When the different elements of utilitarianism are unpackaged, it is seen that

---

[16] On this see Sen (1979a, 1979b, 1985a) and Sen and Williams (1982, 'Introduction').

although a rights-based moral theory cannot coexist with 'welfarism' or 'sum-ranking', it can very well do so with consequentialism.

The second point to note is that it would be a mistake to ignore consequences even when one is dealing with intrinsically valuable objects. The case for consequential reasoning arises from the fact that activities have consequences. Even activities that are intrinsically valuable may have *other* consequences. The intrinsic value of any activity is not an adequate reason for ignoring its instrumental role, and the existence of instrumental relevance is no denial of its intrinsic value. To get an overall assessment of the ethical standing of an activity it is necessary not only to look at its own intrinsic value (if any), but also at its instrumental role and its consequences on other things, i.e. to examine the various intrinsically valuable or disvaluable consequences that this activity may have. What was called the 'engineering' aspect of economics has a parallel within ethics itself. It may not be as central in many ethical problems as it is in mainstream economics, but it can be important enough.

The third point I would like to make is that consequential reasoning may be fruitfully used even when consequentialism as such is not accepted. To ignore consequences is to leave an ethical story half told. Consequentialism, however, demands more than the telling of the story. It demands, in particular, that the rightness of actions be judged entirely by the goodness of consequences, and this is a demand not merely of taking consequences into account, but of ignoring everything else. Of course, the dichotomy can be reduced by seeing consequences in very broad terms, including the value of actions performed or the disvalue of violated rights. I have tried to argue elsewhere:

1 that such broadening is helpful, indeed essential; but
2 that nevertheless even after fully fledged broadening, there can remain a gap between consequentialist evalua-tion and consequence–sensitive deontological assessment (Sen 1982b, 1983c).

To say that action x should be chosen over action y is not the same statement as that the state of affairs resulting from action x, including action x done, is superior to the state of affairs resulting from action y, including action y done. The force of the distinction may get weaker as consequentialism is more and more broadly defined, but the distinction does not disappear even when consequential reasoning is fully pursued and even when actions per-formed are included among the consequences. Consequen-tial analysis may be taken to be necessary, but not sufficient, for many moral decisions.[17]

The fourth point to note is that consequential reasoning – and indeed consequentialism itself – can be combined with 'position-relativity' of evaluation of states of affairs (Sen 1983c). It is a matter of internal structure of an ethical approach to insist, or *not* to insist, that different persons, irrespective of their positions, must evaluate the same state of affair in exactly the same way. It is possible to take different views on the question as to whether, say, Othello must evaluate the state of affairs in which Desdemona has been killed (as it happens by him) in exactly the same way

---

[17] See Sen (1982b, 1983c, 1985a). Samuel Scheffler (1982) has argued persuasively in favour of distinguishing between the *permission* to do something and an *obligation* to do it, and that consequentialism is much more adequate for the former than for the latter. If some action has the best consequences over-all, it is hard to deny that one is morally free to do that, but it is quite another matter to insist that one is obliged to do exactly that. See also Slote (1985).

as anybody else. The view may be taken, as I have tried to argue it should be, that given Othello's specific position in the state of affairs in question, as Desdemona's lover, husband and killer, a consistent and integrated ethical theory may require Othello to take a far graver view of that state than what others – uninvolved in the matter – can.[18]

If such 'position relativity' in the evaluation of states of affairs is accepted, then various features of agent–relative morality applied to acts, discussed by such philosophers as Bernard Williams, Thomas Nagel and Derek Parfit[19] can be accommodated *within* a consequentialist system (incorporating position-sensitive moral assessment of states of affairs). The advantages of consequential reasoning involving interdependence and instrumental accounting, can be then combined not only with intrinsic valuation, but also with position relativity and agent sensitivity of moral assessment.

It is, of course, true that consequential reasoning appeals to the economists' standard way of looking at prescriptive evaluation, and this can be, and has indeed often been, used rather mechanically. However, if consequential reasoning is used without the additional limitations imposed by the quite different requirements of welfarism, position independence, and the overlooking of possible intrinsic value of instrumentally important variables. then the consequential approach can provide a sensitive as well as

---

[18] This was presented in Sen (1982b), and further analyzed in Sen (1983c, 1985a). See also Regan (1983), Garcia (1986), Steiner (1986).

[19] See Williams (1973a, 1981), Nagel (1979, 1980), and Parfit (1984). I should add in this context that in an interesting paper the criticisms that Philippa Foot (1985) makes of the 'goal-rights systems' proposed in Sen (1982b) seem to depend on not taking adequate note of position-relativity that such systems admit (Sen 1982b, pp. 33–8; see also Sen 1983c).

a robust structure for prescriptive thinking on such matters as rights and freedom. I have also argued that there are distinct advantages in following this route. It contrasts both with the narrow consequentialist welfarism used in standard welfare economics, and also with some deontological approaches used in moral philosophy, involving inadequate consequential accounting.

Ethics and Economics

It is arguable that a closer contact between ethics and economics can be beneficial not only to economics but even to ethics. Many ethical problems have what we have been calling 'engineering' aspects, and some of them do, in fact, involve economic relations. Even Aristotle's analysis of 'the good for man' included, as was discussed in the first lecture, various issues of economic management, with corresponding demands on economic engineering. But aside from direct use of economic reasoning, the tradition in economics of emphasizing and pursuing logistic issues of interdependence and interconnections has some methodological bearing on ethical arguments. I have briefly sketched above the argument for extending some of the contemporary ethical discussions more in the consequential direction, despite the understandable rejection of utilitarianism and its peculiarly narrow form of consequential accounting.

In these lectures I have, however, been more concerned with what ethics can do for economics than with its converse. I have tried to argue that the distancing of economics from ethics has impoverished welfare economics, and also weakened the basis of a good deal of descriptive and predictive economics. In the earlier lectures, the indirect effects of the impoverishment of welfare economics on descriptive and predictive economics were discussed. I come back to that question now, at the end of this last lecture.

The wide use of the extremely narrow assumption of self-interested behaviour has, I have tried to argue, seriously limited the scope of predictive economics, and made it difficult to pursue a number of important economic relationships that operate through behavioural versatility. As discussed in the last lecture and this one, the richness of ethical considerations in welfare–economic evaluation has a direct bearing on personal behaviour. It is not my intention to suggest that no behavioural model can be useful unless it took note of all these complexities. Obviously, many shortcuts have to be pursued, and the predictive relevance of the different types of ethical considerations have to be correspondingly examined. On the other hand, sticking entirely to the narrow and implausible assumption of purely self-interested behaviour seems to take us in an alleged 'short-cut' that ends up in a different place from where we wanted it to go. The object is to understand, explain and predict human behaviour in a way such that economic relationships can be fruitfully studied and used for description, prognosis and policy. The jettisoning of all motivations and valuations other than the extremely narrow one of self-interest is hard to justify on grounds of predictive usefulness, and it also seems to have rather dubious empirical support. To stick to that narrow path does not seem a very good way of going about our business.

There is, however, a complexity in the formulation of 'self-interested behaviour', which I have not yet discussed, and which may be quite important for understanding the nature of the challenge involved in getting a deeper insight into the relationship between self-interest and behaviour.

Welfare, Goals and Choices

In the usual economic literature a person is seen as maximizing his utility function, which depends only on his own consumption, and which determines all his choices. This complex structure of 'self-interested behaviour' has three distinct – and essentially independent – features.

Self-centred welfare: A person's welfare depends only on his or her own consumption (and in particular it does not involve any sympathy or antipathy towards others).

Self-welfare goals: a person's goal is to maximize his or her own welfare, and – given uncertainty – the probability-weighted expected value of that welfare (and in particular, it does not involve directly attaching importance to the welfare of others).

Self-goal choice: Each act of choice of a person is guided immediately by the pursuit of one's own goal (and in particular, it is not restrained or adapted by the recognition of mutual interdependence of respective successes, given other people's pursuit of their goals).[20]

In standard economic theory (e.g. in mainline general equilibrium analysis), all these three assumptions are simultaneously made, and compounded together. But it is possible to separate them out. For example, a person's welfare may not depend only on his own consumption, even though his only goal may be maximization of his own welfare, and all his choices may reflect that goal (see, for example, Winter 1969; Archibald and Donaldson 1976).

---

[20] These distinctions and their relevance have been investigated in Sen (1985d).

Or, a person's welfare may depend only on his own consumption, but his goals may involve objectives other than maximizing his own welfare only (see, for example, Akerlof 1983). Various types of departures from self-interested behaviour can be found in terms of violations of any one, any two, or all three of these distinct requirements (see Sen 1985d).

Attaching importance to welfare–economic consideration may have the effect of making the person violate these requirements. Ethical considerations might suggest maximizing some objective other than one's welfare, and can also induce responses that make personal welfare rest on a base wider than one's own consumption. The implications of different ethical considerations on these distinct features incorporated in self-interested behaviour can be systematically worked out.

The feature that is hardest to deal with is that of *self-goal choice*. Indeed, that a person can be expected to choose whichever alternative course of action is best suited to serve his or her goals (including moral objectives if any), given other things on which he or she has no control (including the choices of others), might seem to be entirely reasonable – perhaps even unexceptionable.

The real difficulty with the assumption of self-goal choice arises not from any lack of immediate intuitive plausibility, but rather from the fact that the use of self-goal choice on the part of a community of people with diverse goals may lead to each person's goals being less fulfilled than they would have been had the persons followed a different rule of behaviour. Problems of this type can be easily characterized in terms of some standard games, e.g. Prisoners' Dilemma (see Luce and Raiffa 1957; Olson 1965; Parfit 1984).[21] These games are, of course, artificial, but they

---

[21] See also Baumol (1952), Sen (1961, 1967a, 1974), Marglin (1963),

relate quite closely to various real-life problems – including many economic ones – and draw our attention to major issues in social conduct.

In the Prisoners' Dilemma each person has a 'strictly dominant' individual strategy, in the sense that no matter what others do, each person's own goals are better served by following that dominant (and 'self-goal') strategy. At the same time, everyone's goals would have been respectively better served had they followed a different (and more cooperative) strategy. Given 'self-goal' choice, it is clear that each person will indeed follow the non-cooperative strategy, and thereby everyone will end up in a situation inferior to following the cooperative strategy.[22] There are

---

Watkins (1974, 1985), Taylor (1976), Weymark (1978), Doel (1979), Hardin (1982), Bacharach (1985), Campbell and Snowden (1985), Gauthier (1986), for illustrations of the nature of the problem involved in a 'Prisoners' Dilemma' situation.

[22] Note that a 'Prisoners' Dilemma' situation can arise even when both the players are very 'moral' and not simply maximizing their respective well-beings (on this see Parfit 1984). In fact, it can be readily checked that what is crucial for the Prisoners' Dilemma is 'self-goal choice' rather than either 'self-centred welfare' or 'self-welfare goal'. Two persons with different moral goal-orderings can be involved in a Prisoners' Dilemma game, and if they both pursue self-goal choice, then all the usual results will follow. This is not to be interpreted to mean that there is no moral solution to the Prisoners' Dilemma, since morality is not merely a matter of having one set of goals rather than another, but also of the relation between action and conduct, on the one hand, and goals, aims, values, etc., on the other. The issue of the correspondence between goals and choice arises not merely in the general context of consequentialism (see Williams 1973), but also in that of assessing the action implications of one's own goals in the light of the goals of others (see Sen 1974, 1983a; Gauthier 1986). In particular, the need for considering the metaranking of one's possible rankings arises even when the latter are different moral orderings, rather than reflections of, say, personal well-being. For different types of concepts of metarankings and their critical examinations, see

real-life analogies of this kind of problem in many areas of real importance in economics, e.g. achieving high industrial productivity, which may depend on the efforts of all, even though each person may be able to serve his or her own goals better by abstaining from intense application (while enjoying the fruits of other people's work).

Experimental studies of game-theoretic behaviour have also tended to reveal departures from self-goal choice (see, for example, Lave 1962, Rapoport and Chammah 1965, Axelrod 1984). Such departures are quite clearly noticed also in real-life experiences, involving economic and social matters. There is evidence of people following certain rules of behaviour that go against the goals they acknowledge and eventually wish to maximize, and this sometimes happens without their attaching any *intrinsic* importance to following these rules of behaviour. Such rules may, in fact, be followed for instrumental reasons, for the benefit of the group as a whole in the form of the goals of *each* being better served, even though each person might have been able to enhance the fulfilment of his or her own goals further by following a different strategy, *given* the strategy choice of others.

In recent years there has developed a fairly extensive game-theoretic literature in dealing with the prevalence of cooperative behaviour in *finitely repeated* Prisoners' Dilemma games. This is interesting and important since there is a general argument against such cooperation in finitely repeated Prisoners' Dilemma. The argument is that any

---

Frankfurt 1971, Jeffrey 1974, Sen 1974, 1977c, Baier 1977, Baigent 1980, Majumdar 1980, Pattanaik 1980, Hollis 1981, Van der Veen 1981, Hirschman 1982, McPherson 1982, 1984, Schelling 1984, Schick 1984). The general point about the low informational content of *one* chosen ranking applies to moral rankings as well (Sen, 1984a).

reward from not pursuing self-goal choice must arise from the favourable response of other players in later rounds. Clearly, there is no case, therefore, for departing from self-goal choice in the *last* round, since there are no later rounds. But since each party has no incentive to depart from self-goal choice in the last round, there is no point in selfless behaviour in the *last-but-one* round either, since no-one will respond in the last round anyway. Inducing backwards, it can be shown, on the basis of this type of reasoning, that there will be no case for departing from self-goal choice at any stage of the game. The fact is, nevertheless, that cooperation does seem to emerge in these games.

In the formal literature, there have been various attempts to explain the emergence of cooperation by introducing some kind of a 'defect' in either the knowledge, or the reasoning of the players. The players could be ignorant as to how many times the game would be played, thereby making the backward induction impossible. Or, the players may not know fully what the other players' objective or knowledge happens to be, and they may entertain the belief – falsely as it happens – that others would actually enjoy cooperation and respond accordingly. Or the possible behaviour patterns that may be considered may be arbitrarily limited in some special way without all variational possibilities being examined.[23]

These 'defects' may indeed be present, but it is also possible that cooperative behaviour has quite a different explanation. Indeed, such cooperation is often found even in *non-repeated* games of this type, in one-off real-life

---

[23] See the interesting contributions of Taylor (1976), Basu (1977), Radner (1980), Smale (1980), Axelrod (1981, 1984), Hardin (1982), Kreps, Milgrom, Roberts and Wilson (1982).

situations. It could, of course, be the case that the real goals of a person are not the ones that they believe they are trying to maximize. But it is also possible that people clearly understand their goals, wish to maximize them, but nevertheless take note of other people's goals, due to a recognition of the nature of mutual interdependence of the achievements of different people in these situations.[24]

Behaviour is ultimately a social matter as well, and thinking in terms of what 'we' should do, or what should be 'our' strategy, may reflect a sense of identity involving recognition of other people's goals and the mutual interdependencies involved. Even though other people's goals may not be incorporated in one's own goals, the recognition of interdependence may suggest following certain rules of behaviour, which are not necessarily of intrinsic value, but which are of great *instrumental* importance in the enhancement of the respective goals of the members of that group.

The language of game theory – and indeed of economic theory – makes it hard to discuss behaviour patterns of this kind, since it is very tempting to think that whatever a person may appear to be maximizing, on a simple interpretation, must be that person's goal. But what a person can be seen as maximizing depends on a certain reading of what he or she takes to be the appropriate control variables and what variations are seen as the right means of control exercised by each player. There is a genuine ambiguity here when the instrumental value of certain *social* rules are accepted for the *general* pursuit of

---

[24] See Sen (1973a, 1974), Watkins (1974, 1985), Ullman-Margalit (1977), Levi (1982), Binmore (1984), Parfit (1984). On related matters regarding the nature of social convention, see the alternative interpretations of Lewis (1969) and Gilbert (1983).

individual goals. If reciprocity is not taken to be intrinsically important, but instrumentally so, and that recognition is given expression in actual reciprocal behaviour, for achieving each person's own goals better, it is hard to argue that the person's 'real goal' is to follow reciprocity rather than their respective actual goals.

This way of looking at the problem of cooperation in Prisoners' Dilemma has some advantages over the other approaches.[25] For one thing, this applies also to non-repeated Prisoners' Dilemma, and many real-life cases of cooperative behaviour seem to be like that. Second, it does not have the problem of finding a solution by incorporating some kind of a 'defect' in knowledge. It may be that people are often ignorant, but a model of 'rational' behaviour that counts on ignorance for being able to achieve good results, which will fail to be realized if people become better informed, has an element of perversity in it.

Of course it must be admitted that there are ambiguities also in the conception of social instrumentality, but it is a route that does have some plausibility. Indeed, the possibility of incompleteness or overdeterminacy discussed earlier in this lecture in the context of conflicts of principles has some relevance to this ambiguity. If the person sees actions in terms of social strategy, taking note of the respective goals of others similarly placed in the Prisoners' Dilemma game, then following the cooperative strategy does have some appropriateness: 'It is better for the respective goals of all of us.' If on the other hand, each person thinks only in terms of self-goal choice and sees nothing wrong in assuming – when making strategy-choice – that the actions of others are *given* (irrespective of their own actions), then

---

[25] I have tried to explore this line of analysis and some of its implications in Sen (1985d, 1986d).

the dominant strategy of non-cooperative behaviour is indeed quite compelling: 'It is better respectively for each of us, given what others do.' The two alternative bases of behaviour are both quite deep, and both have excellent reasons for suggesting the respective courses of action. Whether this dilemma is treated as one to be fully resolved one way or the other (in line with 'balanced complete ordering'), or left as a case of incompleteness ('there is no compelling reason for either course'), or seen as illustrating overcompleteness ('there are compelling reasons for each of the two courses, but they conflict'), is not as important as recognizing that there is a genuine ambiguity here as to what reason does dictate.[26]The case for accepting the instrumental role of social behaviour, which goes against each person's dominant strategy, is not easy to dismiss, and it is not at all clear why group-rationality considerations of this type may not influence actual behaviour without invoking any 'defects' in people's knowledge. Thus the observations from experimental games, or from real life, may not be so counterintuitive after all.

Indeed, even Adam Smith had pointed to the instrumental importance of 'rules of conduct': 'Those general rules of conduct, when they have been fixed in our mind by habitual reflection, are of great use in correcting misrepresentation of self-love concerning what is fit and proper to be done in our particular situation' (Smith 1790, p. 160). There is a complex instrumental ethics involved in such social morality. In such problems as pursuing industrial

---

[26] This ambiguity is not an embarrassment. In fact, even the actual outcomes in 'Prisoners' Dilemma' situations do vary. The inescapable conflict of two powerful principles makes ambiguity about the demands of rationality hard to avoid.

relations, achieving productivity within the enterprise, and a variety of other economic exercises, this type of behaviour may well be important.[27]

Conduct, Ethics and Economics

One of the interesting points to emerge from the foregoing analyses is that departures from standard behavioural

---

[27] Arguments have been presented by 'indirect utilitarians' (especially by Harsanyi 1982, 1983, and Hare 1981, 1982) for incorporating adherence to rules *within* utilitarian calculus itself, adapting the format of 'rule utilitarianism'. This move has much merit in broadening the scope of utilitarian arguments, and for avoiding some of the special follies of act-based utilitarianism (on which see Gibbard 1965). But some serious problems must also be noted. First, the 'welfarism' implicit in 'rule utilitarianism', which is essentially an amalgam of 'rule consequentialism' and 'welfarism', limits the scope of this extension, since individuals may not, in fact, assess states of affairs in terms of utility information only. Second, 'rule utilitarianism' of any kind can sometimes produce *worse* states than would have emerged from act-based reasoning (the 'rule' acting as an inefficient constraint). Examples of such cases are indeed very plausible (see Lyons 1982). Harsanyi's (1977) particular formalization of 'rule utilitarianism', which depends on some basic symmetry in the positions of different individuals, may be counterproductive in asymmetric circumstances. Neither a general adherence to 'act consequentialism', nor to 'rule consequentialism', can 'work' in all circumstances – indeed no 'single-focus consequentialism' can (Sen 1979b). On related matters, see Regan (1980) and Parfit (1984). What may be called 'social rationality' requires a more parametric formulation, taking more explicit note of the contingent social circumstances – in particular of the nature of symmetry or asymmetry that obtains in the relations of actions, consequences and valuations. I have tried to investigate some of these issues in a forthcoming monograph (tentatively called 'Rationality and Society'), to be published by Harvard University Press and Basil Blackwell.

assumptions of economic theory – incorporating all the three components of self-centred behaviour – may arise from many distinct ethical considerations. They may involve bonhomie and sympathy for others. There may also be commitments to various causes. Further, there may be commitment to particular behaviour patterns, the violation of which may be seen to be intrinsically bad. But there may be also other behaviour patterns, loyalty to which may not arise from any intrinsic valuation related to that behaviour itself, but from the instrumental importance of that behaviour – either individually or for the group. This last consideration may be relevant even in some standard economic cases of failure of efficiency arising from externalities (or non-market interdependences). The incentive problems in tackling these externalities may have to be reformulated altogether if departures from self-interested behaviour – involving the violation of any of the three elements specified – can be systematically admitted into economic analysis.

I must stop here. I have tried to argue that welfare economics can be substantially enriched by paying more attention to ethics, and that the study of ethics can also benefit from a closer contact with economics. I have also argued that even predictive and descriptive economics can be helped by making more room for welfare–economic considerations in the determination of behaviour. I have not tried to argue that either of these exercises would be particularly easy. They involve deep-seated ambiguities, and many of the problems are inherently complex. But the case for bringing economics closer to ethics does not rest on this being an easy thing to do. The case lies, instead, on the rewards of the exercise. I have argued that the rewards can be expected to be rather large.

References

Ackerman, B.A. 1980: *Social Justice in the Liberal State*. New Haven, Conn.: Yale University Press.

Adelman, I. 1975: Development economics – a reassessment of goals. *American Economic Review*, 65.

Ahluwalia, M.S. 1978: Rural poverty and agricultural performance in India. *Journal of Development Studies*, 14.

Aigner, D.J. and Heins, A.J. 1967: A social welfare view of the measurement of income inequality. *Review of Income and Wealth*, 13.

Aizerman, M.A. 1985: New problems in the general choice theory: review of a research trend. *Social Choice and Welfare*, 2.

Akerlof, G.A. 1983: Loyalty Filters. *American Economic Review*, 73.

Akerlof, G.A. 1984: *An Economic Theorist's Book of Tales*. Cambridge: University Press.

Akerlof, G.A. and Dickens, W.T. 1982: The economic consequences of cognitive dissonance. *American Economic Review*, 72.

Aldrich, J. 1977: The dilemma of a Paretian liberal: some consequences of Sen's theorem. *Public Choice*, 30.

Allais, M. 1953: Le Comportement de l'Homme Rationnel devant le Risque: Critique de Postulats et Axiomes de l'Ecole Americaine. *Econometrica*, 21.

Allais, M. and Hagen, O. (eds) 1979: *Expected Utility Hypothesis and the Arrow Paradox*. Dordrecht: Reidel.

Anand, S. 1977: Aspects of poverty in Malaysia. *Review of Income and Wealth*, 23.

Anand, S. 1983: *Inequality and Poverty in Malaysia*. New York: Oxford University Press.

Archibald, G.C. and Donaldson, D. 1976: Non-paternalism and

the basic theorems of welfare economics. *Canadian Journal of Economics*, 9.

Archibald, G.C. and Donaldson, D. 1979: Notes on economic inequality. *Journal of Public Economics*, 12.

Aristotle, *The Nicomachean Ethics*; English translation, Ross (1980).

Aristotle, *Politics*; English translation, Barker (1958).

Arrow, K.J. 1951a: *Social Choice and Individual Values*. New York.

Arrow, K.J. 1951b: An extension of the basic theorems of classic welfare economics. In J. Neyman (ed.), *Proceedings of the Second Berkeley Symposium of Mathematical Statistics*, Berkeley, Calif.: University of California Press.

Arrow, K.J. 1959: Rational choice functions and orderings. *Economica*, 26.

Arrow, K.J. 1963: *Social Choice and Individual Values*, 2nd (extended) edition, New York: Wiley.

Arrow, K.J. 1973: Some ordinalist-utilitarian notes on Rawls's theory of justice. *Journal of Philosophy*, 70.

Arrow, K.J. 1977: Extended sympathy and the possibility of social choice. *American Economic Review*, 67.

Arrow, K.J. 1982: Risk perception in psychology and economics. *Economic Inquiry*, 20.

Arrow, K.J. 1983: Behaviour under uncertainty and its implications for policy, in Stigum and Wenstop (1983).

Arrow, K.J. and Hahn, F.H. 1971: *General Competitive Analysis*. San Francisco: Holden-Day; republished, Amsterdam: North-Holland, 1979.

Atkinson, A.B. 1970: On the measurement of inequality, *Journal of Economic Theory*, 2 (reprinted in Atkinson 1983).

Atkinson, A.B. 1975: *The Economics of Inequality*. Oxford: Clarendon Press.

Atkinson, A.B. 1983: *Social Justice and Public Policy*. Brighton: Wheatsheaf; and Cambridge, Mass.: MIT Press.

Atkinson, A.B. and Bourguignon, F. 1982: The comparison of multidimensional distributions of economic status. *Review of Economic Studies*, 49.

Aumann, R.J. and Kurz, M. 1977: Power and taxes, *Econometrica*, 45.

Austen-Smith, D. 1979: Fair rights. *Economic Letters*, 4.

Austen-Smith, D. 1982: Restricted Pareto and rights. *Journal of Economic Theory*, 26.

Axelrod, R. 1981: The Emergence of Cooperation among Egoists. *American Political Science Review*, 75.

Axelrod, R. 1984: The Evolution of Cooperation. New York: Academic Press.

Bacharach, M. 1985: *A Theory of Rational Decisions in Games*, mimeographed, Christ Church, Oxford.

Baier, K. 1977: Rationality and morality, *Erkenntnis*, 11.

Baigent, N. 1980: Social choice correspondences, *Recherches Economiques de Louvain*, 46.

Bardhan, P. 1984: *Land, labour and rural poverty*. New York: Columbia University Press.

Barker, E. 1958: *The Politics of Aristotle*. London: Oxford University Press.

Barnes, J. 1980: Freedom, rationality and paradox, *Canadian Journal of Philosophy*, 10.

Barry, B. 1986: "Lady Chatterley's Lover and Doctor Fischer's Bomb Party: Liberalism, Pareto Optimality, and the Problem of Objectionable Preferences," in Elster and Hylland (1986).

Basu, K. 1977: Information and strategy in iterated prisoners' dilemma. *Theory and Decision*, 8.

Basu, K. 1979: *Revealed preference of the Government*. Cambridge: University Press.

Basu, K. 1984: The right to give up rights. *Economica, 51*.

Batra, R. and Pattanaik, P.K. *1972:* On some suggestions for having non-binary social choice functions. *Theory and Decision*, 3.

Baumol, W.J. 1952: *Welfare Economics and the Theory of the State*. Cambridge, Mass.: Harvard University Press; 2nd edition, 1966.

Becker G.S. 1976: *The Economic Approach to Human Behaviour*. Chicago: University Press.

Becker G.S. 1981: *A Treatise on the Family*. Cambridge, Mass.: Harvard University Press.

Becker, G.S. 1983: A theory of competition among pressure groups for political influence. *Quarterly Journal of Economics*, 98.

Bell, D.E. 1982: Regret in decision making under uncertainty. *Operations Research*, 30.

Bell, D. and Kristol, I. 1981: *The Crisis in Economic Theory*. New York: Basic Books.

Bentzel, R. 1970: The Social Significance of Income Distribution Statistics. *Review of Income and Wealth*, 16.

Bergson, A. 1938: A reformulation of certain aspects of welfare economics, *Quarterly Journal of Economics*, 52.

Bergstrom, T. 1970: A 'Scandinavian consensus' solution for efficient income distribution among nonmalevolent consumers. *Journal of Economic Theory*, 2.

Berlin, I. 1978: *Concepts and Categories*. Oxford: University Press.

Bernholz, P. 1974: Is a Paretian liberal really impossible? *Public Choice*, 19.

Bernholz, P. 1980: A general social dilemma: profitable exchange and intransitive group preferences. *Zeitschrift für Nationalökonomie*, 40.

Bezembinder, Th. and van Acker, P. 1986: Factual versus Representational Utilities and Their Interdimensional Comparisons, mimeographed, Catholic University, Nijmegen.

Bhattacharya, N. and Chatterjee, G.S. 1977: A further note on between state variations in levels of living in India, mimeographed. Forthcoming in Srinivasan and Bardhan (1986).

Bigman, D. 1986: *On the Measurement of Poverty and Deprivation*, Mimeographed, Hebrew University of Jerusalem.

Binmore, K. 1984: *Game Theory*. To be published. London: School of Economics.

Blackorby, C. 1975: Degrees of cardinality and aggregate partial ordering. *Econometrica*, 43.

Blackorby, C. and Donaldson, D. 1977: Utility versus equity: some plausible quasiorderings. *Journal of Public Economics*, 7.

Blackorby, C. and Donaldson, D. 1978: Measures of relative equality and their meanings in terms of social welfare, *Journal of Economic Theory*, 18.

Blackorby, C. and Donaldson, D. 1980: Ethical indices for the measurement of poverty. *Econometrica*, 48.

Blackorby, C. and Donaldson D. 1984: Ethically significant ordinal indexes of relative inequality, *Advances in Econometrics*, 3.

Blackorby, C., Donaldson, D. and Weymark, J. 1984: Social choice with interpersonal utility comparisons: a diagrammatic introduction. *International Economic Review*, 25.

Blair, D.H. and Pollak, R.A. 1983: Rational collective choice. *Scientific American*, 249 (April).

Blau, J.H. 1975: Liberal values and independence. *Review of Economic Studies*, 42.

Blau, J.H. 1976: Neutrality, monotonicity and the right of veto: a comment. *Econometrica*, 44.

Blaug, M. 1980: *The Methodology of Economics*. Cambridge: University Press.

Boadway, R.W. and Bruce, N. 1984: *Welfare Economics*. Oxford: Blackwell.

Bohm, P. and Kneese, A.V., eds. 1971. *The Economics of Environment*. London: Macmillan.

Borch, K. and Mossin, J. 1968: *Risk and Uncertainty*. London: Macmillan.

Bose, A. 1975: *Marxian and Post-Marxian Political Economy*. Harmondsworth: Penguin Books.

Bourguignon, F. 1979: Decomposable income inequality measures. *Econometrica*, 47.

Brams, S.J. 1975: *Game Theory and Politics*. New York: Free Press.

Brenkert, G.G. 1983: *Marx's Ethics of Freedom*, London: Routledge and Kegan Paul.

Brennan, G. and Lomasky, L. 1985: The impartial spectator goes to Washington: Toward a Smithian theory of electoral behavior. *Economics and Philosophy*, 1.

Breyer, F. 1977: The liberal paradox, decisiveness over issues, and domain restrictions. *Zeitschrift für Nationalökonomie*, 37.

Breyer, F. and Gardner, R. 1980: Liberal paradox, game equilibrium, and Gibbard optimum, *Public Choice*, 35.

Breyer, F. and Gigliotti, G.A. 1980: Empathy and the respect for the right of others. *Zeitschrift für Nationalökonomie*, 40.

Brittan, S. 1983: *The Role and Limits of Government: Essays in Political Economy*. London: Temple Smith.

Broder, I.E. and Morris, C.T. 1982: Socially weighted real income comparisons: an application to India. *World Development*.

Broome, J. 1978: Choice and value in economics. *Oxford Economic Papers*, 30.

Broome, J. 1984: Uncertainty and fairness. *Economic Journal*, 94.

Brown, D.J. 1975: Aggregation of preferences. *Quarterly Journal of Economics*, 89.

Buchanan, A.E. 1982: *Marx on Justice: The Radical Critique of Liberalism*. London: Methuen.

Buchanan, J.M. 1975: *The Limits of Liberty*. Chicago: University Press.

Buchanan, J.M. 1986: *Liberty, Market and the State*. Brighton: Wheatsheaf Books.

Buchanan, J.M. and Tullock, G. 1962: *The Calculus of Consent*. Ann Arbor: University of Michigan Press.

Calabresi, G. and Bobbitt, P. 1978: *Tragic Choices*. New York: Norton.

Campbell, D.E. 1976: Democratic preference functions. *Journal of Economic Theory*, 12.

Campbell, R. and Sowden, L. 1985: *Paradoxes of Rationality and Cooperation*. Vancouver: UBC Press.

Chakravarty, S.R. 1983a: Ethically flexible measures of poverty. *Canadian Journal of Economics*, 16.

Chakravarty, S.R. 1983b: Measures of poverty based on income gap, *Sankhya*, 45.

Chakravarty, Sukhamoy 1969: *Capital and Development Planning*. Cambridge, Mass.: MIT Press.

Chapman, B. 1983: Rights as constraints: Nozick versus Sen. *Theory and Decision*, 15.

Chichilnisky, G. 1980: Basic needs and global models: resources, trade and distribution. *Alternatives*, 6.

Chichilnisky, G. and Heal, G. 1983: Necessary and sufficient conditions for a resolution of the social choice paradox. *Journal of Economic Theory*, 31.

Chipman, J.S., Hurwicz, L., Richter, M.K. and Sonnenschein, H.F. 1971: *Preference, Utility and Demand*. New York: Harcourt.

Clark, S., Hemming, R. and Ulph, D. 1981: On indices for the measurement of poverty. *Economic Journal*, 91.

Cohen, G.A. 1978: *Karl Marx's Theory of History: A Defence*. Oxford: Clarendon Press.

Collard, D. 1975: Edgeworth's propositions on altruism. *Economic Journal*, 85.

Collard, D. 1978: *Altruism and Economy*. Oxford: Martin Robertson.

Cowell, F.A. 1977: *Measuring Inequality*. New York: Wiley.

Daboni, L., Montesano, A. and Lines, M. (eds) 1986: *Recent Developments in the Foundations of Utility and Risk Theory.* Dordrecht: Reidel.

Dalton, H. 1920: The measurement of inequality of incomes. *Economic Journal*, 30.

Daniels, N., ed. 1975: *Reading Rawls.* Oxford: Blackwell.

Dasgupta, A.K. 1985: *Epochs of Economic Theory.* Oxford: Blackwell.

Dasgupta, P. 1982a: *The Control of Resources.* Oxford: Blackwell.

Dasgupta, P. 1982b: Utilitarianism, information and rights, in Sen and Williams (1982).

Dasgupta, P. 1986: Positive freedom, markets and the welfare state. *Oxford Review of Economic Policy*, 2.

Dasgupta, P. and Heal, G. 1979: *Economic Theory and Exhaustible Resources.* London: James Nisbet, and Cambridge: University Press.

Dasgupta, P., Hammond, P. and Maskin, E. 1979: The implementation of social choice rules: some general results on incentive compatibility. *Review of Economic Studies*. 46.

Dasgupta, P., Sen, A. and Starrett, D. 1973: Notes on the measurement of inequality, *Journal of Economic Theory*, 6.

d'Aspremont, C. 1985: Axioms for social welfare orderings, in Hurwicz, Schmeidler and Sonnenschein (1985).

d'Aspremont, C. and Gevers, L. 1977: Equity and informational basis of collective choice. *Review of Economic Studies*, 44.

Davidson, D. 1985a: *Essays on Actions and Events.* Oxford: Clarendon Press.

Davidson D. 1985b: A new basis for decision theory, *Theory and Decision*, 18; also in Daboni, Montesano and Lines (1986).

Davidson, D. 1986: Judging interpersonal interests, in Elster and Hylland (1986).

Davidson, D., Suppes, P. and Siegel, S. 1957: *Decision Making: An Experimental Approach.* Stanford: University Press.

Dawkins, R. 1976: *The Selfish Gene.* Oxford: Clarendon Press.

Dawkins, R. 1982: *The Extended Phenotype.* Oxford: Clarendon Press.

Deaton, A. and Muellbauer, J. 1980: *Economics and Consumer Behaviour.* Cambridge: University Press.

Debreu, G. 1959: *Theory of Value.* New York: Wiley.

Deschamps, R. and Gevers, L. 1978: Leximin and utilitarian rules: a joint characterisation. *Journal of Economic Theory*, 17.

Diwan, R. and Lutz, M. 1985: *Essays in Gandhian Economics.* New Delhi: Gandhi Peace Foundation.

Doel, H. van den 1979: *Democracy and Welfare Economics.* Cambridge: University Press.

Donaldson, D. and Weymark, J. 1986: Properties of fixed-population poverty indices. *International Economic Review,* 27.

Dore, R. 1983: Goodwill and the spirit of market capitalism. *British Journal of Sociology,* 34.

Dore, R. 1984: *Authority and Benevolence: The Confucian Recipe for Industrial Success.* The McCallum Lecture, Pembroke College, Oxford.

Douglas, J. 1983: *Why Charity? The Case for a Third Sector.* London: Sage.

Dummett, M. 1984: *Voting Procedures.* Oxford: Clarendon Press.

Dutta, B. 1978: On the Measurement of Poverty in Rural India. *Indian Economic Review,* 13.

Dutta, B. 1980: Intersectoral disparities and incomes distribution in India: 1960–61 to 1973–74. *Indian Economic Review,* 15.

Dworkin, R. 1978: *Taking Rights Seriously,* 2nd edition. London: Duckworth.

Dworkin, R. 1981: What is equality? Part 1: Equality of Welfare, and What is Equality? Part 2: Equality of Resources. *Philosophy and Public Affairs,* 10.

Dyke, C. 1981: *Philosophy of Economics.* Englewood Cliffs, N.J.: Prentice-Hall.

Ebert, U. 1985: *Measurement of Inequality: An Attempt at Unification and Generalization,* Discussion Paper A-23, University of Bonn.

Edgeworth, F. 1881: *Mathematical Psychics: An Essay on the Application of Mathematics to the Moral Sciences.* London: Kegan Paul.

Eichorn, W. and Gehrig, W. 1982: Measurement of inequality in economics. In B. Korte (ed.), *Modern Applied Mathematics: Optimization and Operations Research.* Amsterdam: North-Holland.

Elster, J. 1978: *Logic and Society.* New York: Wiley.

Elster, J. 1979: *Ulysses and the Sirens.* Cambridge: University Press.

Elster, J. 1983: *Sour Grapes.* Cambridge: University Press.

Elster, J. 1986: *Making Sense of Marx.* Cambridge: Cambridge University Press.

Elster, J. and Hylland, A. (eds) 1986: *Foundations of Social Choice Theory*. Cambridge: University Press.

Farrell, M.J. 1976: Liberalism in the theory of social choice. *Review of Economic Studies*, 43.

Feinberg, J. 1980: *Rights, Justice, and the Bounds of Liberty*. Princeton: University Press.

Feldman, A. 1980: *Welfare Economics and Social Choice Theory*. Boston: Martinus Nijhoff.

Feldman, A. and Kirman, A. 1974: Fairness and envy. *American Economic Review*, 64.

Ferejohn, J.A. 1978: The distribution of rights in society. In Gottinger and Leinfellner (1978).

Fields, G.S. 1980: *Poverty, Inequality, and Development*. Cambridge: University Press.

Fields, G.S. and Fei, J.C.H. 1978: On inequality comparisons. *Econometrica*, 46.

Fine, B.J. 1975a: A note on 'Interpersonal Aggregation and Partial Comparability'. *Econometrica*, 43.

Fine, B.J. 1975b: Individual liberalism in a Paretian society. *Journal of Political Economy*, 83.

Finnis, J. 1983: *Fundamentals of Ethics*. Oxford: Clarendon Press.

Fishburn, P.C. 1973: *The Theory of Social Choice*. Princeton: University Press.

Fishburn, P.C. 1974: Choice functions on finite sets. *International Economic Review*, 15.

Fisher, F.M. 1956: Income distribution, value judgments and welfare. *Quarterly Journal of Economics*, 70.

Fisher, F.M. and Rothenberg, J. 1961: How income ought to be distributed: paradox lost. *Journal of Political Economy*, 69.

Fishkin, J.S. 1979: *Tyranny and Legitimacy*. Baltimore, Md.: Johns Hopkins University Press.

Fishkin, J.S. 1982; *The Limits of Obligation*. New Haven, Conn.: Yale University Press.

Fishkin, J.S. 1983: *Justice, Equal Opportunity and the Family*. New Haven, Conn.: Yale University Press.

Fishkin, J.S. 1984: *Beyond Subjective Morality*. New Haven, Conn.: Yale University Press.

Fishlow, A. *et al.* (eds) 1978: *Rich and Poor Nations in the World Economy*. New York: McGraw-Hill.

Foley, D. 1967: Resource allocation in the public sector. *Yale Economic Essays*, 7.

Foot, P. 1983: Moral realism and moral dilemma. *Journal of Philosophy*, 80.

Foot, P. 1985: Utilitarianism and the virtues. *Mind*, 94.

Foster, J. 1984: On economic poverty: a survey of aggregate measures. *Advances in Econometrics*, 3.

Foster, J. 1986: Inequality measurement. In Young (1986).

Foster, J., Greer, J. and Thorbecke, E. 1984: A class of decomposable poverty measures. *Econometrica*, 42.

Fountain, J. 1980: Bowley's analysis of bilateral monopoly and Sen's liberal paradox in collective choice theory: a note. *Quarterly Journal of Economics*, 95.

Frank. R.H 1985: *Choosing the Right Pond*. New York: Oxford University Press.

Frankfurt, H. 1971: Freedom of the will and the concept of a person. *Journal of Philosophy*, 67.

Frey, B.S. 1983: *Democratic Economic Policy*. Oxford: Martin Robertson.

Fried, C. 1978: *Right and Wrong*, Cambridge, Mass.: Harvard University Press.

Friedman, M. 1953: *Essays in Positive Economics*. Chicago: University Press.

Friedman, M. and Friedman, R. 1980: *Free to Choose*. London: Secker & Warburg.

Frohlick, H. and Oppenheimer, J.A. 1984: Beyond economic man. *Journal of Conflict Resolution*. 28.

Gaertner, W. 1985: Justice constrained libertarian claims and Pareto efficient collective decisions. *Erkenntnis*, 23.

Gaertner, W. 1986: Pareto, independent rights exercising and strategic behaviour. *Journal of Economics: Zeitschrift für Nationalökenomie*, 46.

Gaertner, W. and Krüger, L. 1981: Self-supporting preferences and individual rights: the possibility of Paretian liberalism. *Economica*, 48.

Gaertner, W. and Krüger, L. 1983: Alternative libertarian claims and Sen's paradox. *Theory and Decision*, 15.

Garcia, J.L.A. 1986: Evaluator relativity and the theory of value. *Mind*, 95.

Gärdenfors, P. 1981: Rights, games and social choice. *Nous*, 15.

Gardner, R. 1980: The strategic inconsistency of Paretian liberalism. *Public Choice*, 35.

Gauthier, D. 1986: *Morals by Agreement*. Oxford: Clarendon Press.

George, D. 1984: Meta-Preferences: Reconsidering Contemporary Notions of Free Choice. In J.C. O'Brien, ed., *Festschrift in Honor of George F. Rohrlich*, Volume III. Bradford: MCB University Press.

Gevers, L. 1979: On interpersonal comparability and social welfare orderings. *Econometrica*, 47.

Gibbard, A. 1965: Rule utilitarianism: a merely illusory alternative? *Australasian Journal of Philosophy*, 93.

Gibbard, A. 1973: Manipulation of voting schemes: a general result. *Econometrica*, 41.

Gibbard, A. 1974: A Pareto-consistent libertarian claim. *Journal of Economic Theory*, 7.

Gibbard, A. 1986: Interpersonal comparisons: preference, good, and the intrinsic reward of a life. In Elster and Hylland (1986).

Gilbert, M. 1983: Agreements, Conventions, and Language, *Synthese*.

Goodin, R.E. 1985: *Protecting the Vulnerable*, Chicago: University Press.

Goodin, R.E. 1986: Laundering Preferences. In Elster and Hylland (1986).

Gorman, W.M. 1955: The intransitivity of certain criteria used in welfare economics. *Oxford Economic Papers*, 7.

Gorman, W.M. 1956: The demand for related goods. *Journal Paper J3129*, Iowa Experimental Station, Ames, IA.

Gorman, W.M. 1976: Tricks with utility function. In M.J. Artis and A.R. Nobay (eds), *Essays in Economic Analysis*. Cambridge: University Press.

Gosling, J.C.B. 1969: *Pleasure and Desire*. Oxford: Clarendon Press.

Gottinger, H.W. and Leinfellner, W. (eds) 1978: *Decision Theory and Social Ethics*. Dordrecht: Reidel.

Graaff, J. de v. 1957: *Theoretical Welfare Economics*. Cambridge: University Press.

Graaff, J. de v. 1977: Equity and efficiency as components of general welfare. *South African Journal of Economices*, 45.

Graaff, J. de v. 1985: Normative measurement theory, to be published.

Grant, J.P. 1978: *Disparity Reduction Rates in Social Indicators*. Washington D.C.: Overseas Development Council.

Green, E.T. 1980: Libertarian aggregation of preferences: what the 'Coase theorem' might have said. Social Science Working Paper 315, California Institute of Technology.

Green, J. and Laffont, J.-J. 1979: *Incentives in Public Decision Making*. Amsterdam: North-Holland.

Griffin, J. 1982: Modern utilitarianism. *Revue Internationale de Philosophie*, 36.

Griffin, J. 1986: *Well-being*. Oxford: Clarendon Press.

Griffin, K. 1976: *Land Concentration and Rural Poverty*. London: Macmillan.

Grossbard, A. 1980: The economics of polygomy. In J. Simon and J. Davanzo (eds), *Research in Population Economy*, vol. 2, Greenwich, Conn.: JAI Press.

Groves, T. and Ledyard, J. 1977: Optimal allocation of public goods: a solution to the 'free rider' problem. *Econometrica*, 46.

Guha, A.S. 1972: Neutrality, monotonicity and the right of veto. *Econometrica*, 40.

Guha, A.S. 1981: *An Evolutionary View of Economic Growth*. Oxford: Clarendon Press.

Hahn, F. 1982: On some difficulties of the utilitarian economist. In Sen and Williams (1982).

Hahn, F. and Hollis, M. (eds) 1979: *Philosophy and Economic Theory*, Oxford: University Press.

Haksar, V. 1979: *Equality, Liberty and Perfectionism*. Oxford: Clarendon Press.

Hamada, K., and Takayama, N. 1978: Censored income distributions and the measurement of poverty. *Bulletin of International Statistical Institute*, 47.

Hammond, P.J. 1976a: Equity, Arrow's conditions, and Rawls' difference principle. *Econometrica*, 44.

Hammond, P.J. 1976b: Why ethical measures of inequality need interpersonal comparisons. *Theory and Decision*, 7.

Hammond, P.J. 1977: Dual interpersonal comparisons of utility and the welfare economics of income distribution. *Journal of Public Economics*, 6.

Hammond, P.J. 1978: Economic welfare with rank order price weighting. *Review of Economic Studies*. 45.

Hammond, P.J. 1981: Liberalism, independent rights and the Pareto principle. In J. Cohen (ed.), *Proceedings of the 6th International Congress of Logic, Methodology and Philosophy of Science*. Dordrecht: Reidel.

Hammond, P.J. 1982: Utilitarianism, uncertainty and information. In Sen and Williams (1982).

Hammond, P.J. 1986: Consequentialist social norms for public decisions. In W. Heller, D. Starr and R. Starrett (1986).

Hampshire, S. 1982: Morality and convention. In Sen and Williams (1982).

Hansson, B. 1968: Choice structures and preference relations. *Synthese*, 18.

Hansson, B. 1977: The measurement of social inequality. In R. Butts and J. Hintikka (eds) *Logic, Methodology and Philosophy of Science*. Dordrecht: Reidel.

Hardin, R. 1982: *Collective Action*. Baltimore, Md: Johns Hopkins University Press.

Hardin, R. 1985: Rational choice theories. Mimeographed; to be published in T. Ball (ed.), *Social and Political Inquiry*, forthcoming.

Hare, R.M. 1952: *The Language of Morals*, 2nd edition, 1961. Oxford: Clarendon Press.

Hare, R.M. 1963: *Freedom and Reason*. Oxford: Clarendon Press.

Hare, R.M. 1981: *Moral Thinking: Its Levels, Methods and Point*. Oxford: Clarendon Press.

Hare, R.M. 1982: Ethical theory and utilitarianism. In Sen and Williams (1982).

Harrison, R. (ed.) 1979: *Rational Action*. Cambridge: University Press.

Harrison, R. 1983: *Bentham*. London: Routledge.

Harsanyi, J.C. 1955: Cardinal welfare, individualistic ethics, and interpersonal comparisons of utility. *Journal of Political Economy*, 63.

Harsanyi, J.C. 1976: *Essays in Ethics, Social Behaviour and Scientific Explanation*. Dordrecht: Reidel.

Harsanyi, J.C. 1977: *Rational Behaviour and Bargaining Equilibrium in Games and Social Situations*. Cambridge: University Press.

Harsanyi, J.C. 1982: Morality and the theory of rational behaviour. In Sen and Williams (1982).

Harsanyi, J.C. 1983: *Rule Utilitarianism, Equality and Justice*. Working Paper CP-438, Center for Research in Management Science, University of California at Berkeley.

Hayek, F.A. 1960: *The Constitution of Liberty*. London: Routledge.

Hayek, F.A. 1967: *Studies in Philosophy, Politics and Economics*. London: Routledge.

Heller, W., Starr, R. and Starrett, D. (eds) 1986: *Social choice and Public Decision Making: Essays in Honor of K.J. Arrow*, vol. I. Cambridge: University Press.

Helm, D. 1984: Predictions and causes: a comparison of Friedman and Hicks on methods. *Oxford Economic Papers*, 36.

Helm, D. 1985: *Enforced Maximization*, D.Phil. thesis; to be published by Clarendon Press, Oxford.

Helm, D. 1986: The Assessment: the economic boarders of the state. *Oxford Review of Economic Policy*, 2.

Herzberger, H. 1973: Ordinal preference and rational choice. *Econometrica*, 41.

Hicks, J.R. 1939: *Value and Capital*. Oxford: Clarendon Press.

Hicks, J.R. 1959: A Manifesto. In his *Essays in World Economics*. Oxford: Clarendon Press; reprinted in Hicks (1981).

Hicks, J.R. 1969: *A Theory of Economic History*. Oxford: Clarendon Press.

Hicks, J.R. 1974: Preference and Welfare. In Mitra (1974).

Hicks, J.R. 1981: *Wealth and Welfare*. Oxford: Blackwell.

Hicks, J.R. 1983: A discipline not a science. In J.R. Hicks (ed.) *Classics and Moderns*. Oxford: Blackwell.

Hindess, B. 1983: Rational choice theory and the analysis of political action. *Economy and Society*, 13.

Hirsch, F. 1977: *Social Limits to Growth*. London: Routledge.

Hirshleifer, J. 1977: Economics from a Biological Viewpoint. *Journal of Law and Economcs*. 20.

Hirshleifer, J. 1985: The expanding domain of economics. *American Economic Review*, 75.

Hirschman, A.O. 1970: *Exit, Voice and Loyalty*. Cambridge, Mass.: Harvard University Press.

Hirschman, A.O. 1977: *The Passions and the Interests: Political Arguments for Capitalism before Its Triumph*. Princeton: University Press.

Hirschman, A.O. 1982: *Shifting Involvements*. Princeton: University Press

Hirschman, A.O. 1984: Against parsimony: three easy ways of complicating some categories of economic discourse. *American Economic Review*, 74; shorter version of Hirschman (1985).

Hirschman, A.O. 1985: Against parsimony: three easy ways of complicating some categories of economic discourse. *Economics and Philosophy* 7; the complete text shortened in Hirschman (1984).

Hollander, S. 1973: *The Economics of Adam Smith*. Toronto.

Hollis: M. 1979: Rational man and social science. In Harrison (1979).

Hollis, M. 1981: Economic man and the original sin. *Political Studies*, 29.

Hollis, M. and Nell, E.J. 1975: *Rational Economic Man*. Cambridge: University Press.

Honderich, T. (ed.) 1985: *Morality and Objectivity: A Tribute to J.L. Mackie*. London: Routledge & Kegan Paul.

Hurley, S.L. 1985a: Objectivity and Disagreements. In Honderich (1985).

Hurley, S.L. 1985b: Supervenience and the possibility of coherence. *Mind*, 94.

Hurwicz, L., Schmeidler, D. and Sonnenschein, H. (eds) 1985: *Social Goals and Social Organisation: Essays in Memory of Elisha Pazner*. Cambridge: University Press.

Hylland, A. 1986: The purpose and significance of social choice theory: some general remarks and application to the 'Lady Chatterley problem'. In Elster and Hylland (1986).

James, S. 1982: The duty to relieve suffering. *Ethics*, 93.

Jeffrey, R.C. 1971: On Interpersonal Utility Theory. *Journal of Philosophy*, 68.

Jeffrey, R.C. 1974: Preferences among preferences. *Journal of Philosophy*, 71.

Jorgenson, D.W., Lau, L.J. and Stoker, T.M. 1980: Welfare comparison under exact aggregation. *American Economic Review*, 70.

Jorgenson, D.W. and Slesnick, D.T. 1984a: Inequality in the distribution of individual welfare. *Advances in Econometrics*, 3.

Jorgenson, D.W. and Slesnick, D.T. 1984b: Aggregate consumer behaviour and the measurement of inequality. *Review of Economic Studies*, 51.

Jorgenson, D.W. and Slesnick, D.T. 1986: *Redistribution Policy and the Elimination of Poverty*. Discussion Paper, Harvard Institute for Economic Research.

Kahneman, D. and Tversky A. 1979: Prospect Theory: An Analysis of Decisions under Risk. *Econometrica*, 47.

Kahneman, D., Slovik, P. and Tversky, A. 1982: *Judgment under Uncertainty: Heuristics and Biases*. Cambridge: University Press.

Kakwani, N. 1980a: On a Class of Poverty Measures. *Econometrica*, 48.

Kakwani, N. 1980b: *Income Inequality and Poverty*. New York: Oxford University Press.

Kakwani, N. 1981: Welfare measures: an international comparison. *Journal of Development Economics*, 8.

Kakwani, N. 1986: *Analysing Redistribution Policies*. Cambridge: University Press.

Kaldor, N. 1939: Welfare propositions in economics. *Economic Journal*, 49.

Kanbur, S.M. (Ravi) and Stromberg, J.O. 1986: Income transitions and income distribution dominance. *Journal of Economic Theory*.

Kaneko, M. 1984: On interpersonal utility comparisons. *Social Choice and Welfare*, 1.

Kanger, S. 1957: *New Foundations for Ethical Theory*, Part I, Stockholm.

Kanger, S. 1981: *Human Rights and Their Realization*. Uppsala: Department of Philosophy, University of Uppsala.

Kanger, S. 1972: Law and logic. *Theoria*, 38.

Kanger, S. 1976: *Choice Based on Preference*. Mimeographed, Uppsala University.

Kanger, S. 1985: On realization of human rights. *Acta Philosophica Fennica*, 38.

Kanger, S. and Kanger, H. 1966: Rights and parliamentarianism, *Theoria*, 32.

Karni, E. 1978: Collective Rationality, Unanimity and Liberal Ethics. *Review of Economic Studies*, 45.

Keeney, R.L. and Raiffa, H. 1976: *Decisions with Multiple Objectives*. New York: Wiley.

Kelly, J.S. 1976a: The impossibility of a just liberal. *Economica*, 43.

Kelly, J.S. 1976b: Rights-exercising and a Pareto-consistent libertarian claim. *Journal of Economic Theory*, 13.

Kelly, J.S. 1978: *Arrow Impossibility Theorems*. New York: Academic Press.

Kelsey, D. 1985: The liberal paradox: a generalization. *Social Choice and Welfare*, 1.

Kern, L. 1978: Comparative distribution ethics: an extension of

Sen's examination of the pure distribution problem. In Gottinger and Leinfellner (1978).

Kolm, S. Ch. 1969: The optimum production of social justice. In Margolis and Guitton (1969).

Kolm, S. Ch. 1976: Unequal inequalities. *Journal of Economic Theory*, 12.

Kornai, J. 1971: *Anti-Equilibrium*. Amsterdam: North-Holland.

Kornai, J. 1985: *Contradictions and Dilemmas*. Cambridge, Mass.: MIT Press.

Körner, S. (ed.) 1974: *Practical Reason*. Oxford: Blackwell.

Kreps, D., Milgrom, P., Roberts, J. and Wilson, R. 1982: Rational cooperation in finitely repeated prisoner's dilemma. *Journal of Economic Theory*, 27.

Krishna Rao, M.V. 1979: *Studies in Kautilya*. New Delhi: Munshiram Manoharlal.

Krüger, L. and Gaertner, W. 1983: Alternative libertarian claims and Sen's paradox. *Theory and Decision*, 15.

Kundu, A. and Smith, T.E. 1983: An impossibility theorem on poverty indices. *International Economic Review*, 24.

Kynch, J. and Sen, A. 1983: Indian women: well-being and survival. *Cambridge Journal of Economics*, 7.

Laffont, J.J. (ed.) 1979: *Aggregation and Revealed Preferences*. Amsterdam: North-Holland.

Lancaster, K.J. 1966: A new approach to consumer theory. *Journal of Political economy*, 74.

Lancaster, K.J. 1971: *Consumer Demand: A New Approach*. New York: Columbia University Press.

Latsis, S.J. (ed.) 1976: *Method and Appraisal in Economics*. Cambridge: University Press.

Lave, L.B. 1962: An empirical approach to the prisoner's dilemma game. *Quarterly Journal of Economics*, 76.

Le Breton, M., Trannoy, A. and Uriarte, J.R. 1985: Topological aggregation of inequality preorders. *Social Choice and Welfare*, 2.

Le Grand, J. 1984: Equity as an economic objective. *Journal of Applied Philosophy*, 1.

Leibenstein, H. 1976: *Beyond Economic Man*, Cambridge, Mass.: Harvard University Press.

Lemmon, E.J. 1962: Moral dilemmas. *Philosophical Review*, 71.

Levi, I. 1974: On indeterminate probabilities, *Journal of Philosophy*, 71.

Levi, I. 1982: Liberty and welfare. In Sen and Williams (1982).

Levi, I. 1986a: *Hard Choices*. Cambridge: University Press.

Levi, I. 1986b: The paradoxes of Allais and Ellsberg. *Economics and Philosophy*, 2.

Lewis, D. 1969: *Convention: A Philosophical Study*. Cambridge, Mass.: Harvard University Press.

Lindahl, L. 1977: *Position and Change*. Dordrecht: Reidel.

Lindbeck, A. 1985: Redistribution policies and the expansion of the public sector. *Journal of Public Economics*, 28.

Lindbeck, A. 1986: Stabilization policies in open economies with endogenous politicians. *American Economic Review*, 66.

Lipton, M. 1985: A problem in poverty measurement. *Mathematical Social Sciences*, 10.

Little, I.M.D. 1957: *A Critique of Welfare Economics*. 2nd edition. Oxford: Clarendon Press.

Loomes, G. and Sugden, R. 1982: Regret theory: an alternative theory of rational choice. *Economic Journal*, 92.

Luce, R.D. and Raiffa, H. 1957: *Games and Decisions*, New York: Wiley.

Lukes, S. 1985: *Marxism and Morality*. Oxford: Clarendon Press.

Lyons, D. 1982: Utility and rights. *Nomos*, 24.

Maasoumi, E. 1986: The measurement and decomposition of multidimensional inequality. *Econometrica*, 54.

McClennen, E.F. 1983: Sure thing doubts. In Stigum and Wenstop (1983).

McCloskey, D.N. 1985: *The Rhetoric of Economics*. Madison: University of Wisconsin Press.

MacCrimmon, K.R. 1968: Descriptive and normative implications of decision theory postulates. In Borch and Mossin (1968).

McDowell, J. 1981: Noncognitivism and Rule-following. In S.H. Holtzman and C.M. Leich (eds.), *Wittgenstein: To Follow a Rule*. London: Routledge & Kegan Paul.

McDowell, J. 1985: Values and secondary qualities. In Honderich (1985).

Machina, M. 1981: 'Rational' Decision Making vs. 'Rational' Decision Modelling. *Journal of Mathematical Psychology*, 24.

McKenzie, L. 1959: On the Existence of General Equilibrium for a Competitive Market. *Econometrica*, 27.

Mackie, J.L. 1978: *Ethics: Inventing Right and Wrong*. Harmondsworth: Penguin.

108   References

Mackie, J.L. 1986: The combination of paritally-ordered preferences. In J.L. Mackie, *Persons and Values*. Oxford: Clarendon Press.

McLean, I. 1980: Liberty, equality and the Pareto principle. *Analysis*, 40.

McLellan, D. 1977: *Karl Marx: Selected Writings*. Oxford: University Press.

McMurrin, S. (ed) 1980: *Tanner Lectures on Human Values*, vol. I. Cambridge: University Press.

McPherson, M.S. 1982: Mill's moral theory and the problem of preference change. *Ethics*,

McPherson, M.S. 1984: Economics: on Hirschman, Schelling and Sen. *Partisan Review*, 41.

Majumdar, T. 1980: The rationality of changing choice. *Analyse und Kritik*, 2.

Majumdar, T. 1983: *Investment in Education and Social Choice*. Cambridge: University Press.

Mäler, K.-G. 1974: *Environmental Economics: A Theoretical Enquiry*. Baltimore: Johns Hopkins University Press.

Malinvaud, E. 1961: The analogy between atemporal and intertemporal theories of resource allocation. *Review of Economic Studies*, 28.

Marcus, R.B. 1980: Moral dilemmas and consistency. *Journal of Philosophy*, 77.

Marglin, S.A. 1963: The social rate of discount and the optimal rate of investment. *Quarterly Journal of Economics*, 77.

Margolis, H. 1982: *Selfishness, Altruism and Rationality*. Cambridge: Cambridge University Press.

Margolis, J. and Guitton, H. (eds) 1969: *Public Economics*. London: Macmillan.

Marx, K. 1843: *On the Jewish Question*. English translation in McLellan (1977).

Marx, K. 1844: *The Economic and Philosophic Manuscript of 1844*, English translation. London: Lawrence & Wishart.

Marx, K. 1875: *Critique of the Gotha Programme*, English translation. New York: International Publishers, 1938.

Marx, K. 1883: *Capital: A Critical Analysis of Capitalist Production*. Third edition, English translation. London: Sonnenschein, 1887.

Marx, K. and Engels, F. 1845–6: *The German Ideology*, English translation. New York: International Publishers, 1947.

Maskin, E. 1978: A theorem on utilitarianism. *Review of Economic Studies*, 45.

Matthews, R.C.O. 1981: Morality, competition and efficiency. *Manchester School*.

Matthews, R.C.O. 1984: Darwinism and economic change. *Oxford Economic Papers*, 36.

Maynard Smith, J. 1982: *Evolution and the Theory of Games*. Cambridge: University Press.

Meade, J.E. 1976: *The Just Economy*. London: Allen and Unwin.

Mehran, F. 1976: Linear Measures of Economic Equality. *Econometrica*, 44.

Mill, J.S. 1859: *On Liberty*, Reprinted. Harmondsworth: Penguin, 1974.

Mill, J.S. 1861: *Utilitarianism*, Reprinted. London: Collins/ Fontana, 1962.

Mirrlees, J.A. 1982: The economic uses of utilitarianism. In Sen and Williams (1982).

Mitra, A. ed. 1974: *Economic Theory and Planning: Essays in Honour of A.K. Das Gupta*. Calcutta: Oxford University Press.

Mookherjee, D. and Shorrocks, A. 1982: A decomposition analysis of the trends in UK income inequality. *Economic Journal*, 92.

Morishima, M. 1964: *Equilibrium, Stability and Growth*. Oxford: Clarendon Press.

Morishima, M. 1982: *Why Has Japan 'Succeeded'? Western Technology Japanese Ethos*. Cambridge: University Press.

Morris, M.D. 1979: *Measuring the Conditions of the World's Poor*. Oxford: Pergamon.

Moulin, H. 1983: *The Strategy of Social Choice*. Amsterdam: North-Holland.

Muellbauer, J. 1974: Inequality measures, prices, and household composition. *Review of Economic Studies*, 41.

Muellbauer, J. 1978: Distributional aspects of price comparisons. In R. Stone and W. Peterson (eds), *Economic Contributions to Public Policy*. London: Macmillan.

Mueller, D.C. 1979: *Public Choice*. Cambridge: University Press.

Musgrave, R.A. 1959: *The Theory of Public Finance*. New York: McGraw-Hill.

Myerson, R.B. 1983: Utilitarianism, egalitarianism and the

timing effect in social choice problems. *Econometrica*, 49.

Nagel, T. 1970: *The Possibility of Altruism*. Oxford: Clarendon Press.

Nagel, T. 1979: *Mortal Questions*. Cambridge: University Press.

Nagel, T. 1980: The limits of objectivity. In McMurrin (1980).

Nagel, T. 1986: *The View from Nowhere*. Oxford: Clarendon Press.

Nelson, R.R. and Winter, S.G. 1982: *An Evolutionary Theory of Economic Change*. Cambridge, Mass.: Harvard University Press.

Newbery, D.M.G. 1970: A Theorem on the Measurement of Inequality. *Journal of Economic Theory*, 2.

Ng, Y-K. 1971: The possibility of a Paretian liberal: impossibility theorems and cardinal utility. *Journal of Political Economy*, 79.

Ng, Y-K. 1979: *Welfare Economics*. London: Macmillan.

Ng. Y-K. 1981: Welfarism: a defence against Sen's attack. *Economic Journal*, 91.

Nitzan, S. and Paroush, J. 1985: *Collective Decision Making: An Economic Outlook*. Cambridge: University Press.

Nozick, R. 1973: Distributive justice. *Philosophy and Public Affairs*, 3.

Nozick, R. 1974: *Anarchy, State and Utopia*. Oxford: Blackwell.

Nozick, R. 1985: Interpersonal utility theory. *Social Choice and Welfare*, 2.

Nussbaum, M.C. 1984: Plato on Commensurability and desire. *Proceedings of the Aristotelian Society*, 85.

Nussbaum, M.C. 1985: Aeschylus and practical conflict. *Ethics*, 95.

Nussbaum, M.C. 1986a: *The Fragility of Goodness: Luck and Ethics in Greek Tragedy and Philosophy*. Cambridge: University Press.

Nussbaum, M.C. 1986b: *The Therapy of Desire*. The Martin Classical Lectures 1986; to be published.

Nussbaum, M.C. 1986c: *Nature, Function and Capability: Aristotle on Political Distribution*. Mimeographed, Brown University.

Nygard, F. and Sandstrom, A. 1981: *Measuring Income Inequality*. Stockholm: Almqvist and Wiksell International.

Olson, M. 1965: *The Logic of Collective Action*. Cambridge, Mass.: Harvard University Press.

O'Neill, O. 1986: *Faces of Hunger*. London: Allen and Unwin.

Osmani, S.R. 1982: *Economic Inequality and Group Welfare*. Oxford: Clarendon Press.

Parfit, D. 1984: *Reasons and Persons*. Oxford: Clarendon Press.

Pattanaik, P.K. 1971: *Voting and Collective Choice*. Cambridge: University Press.

Pattanaik, P.K. 1978: *Strategy and Group Choice*. Amsterdam: North-Holland.

Pattanaik, P.K. 1980: A note on the 'rationality of becoming' and revealed preference. *Analyse und Kritik*, 2.

Pattanaik, P.K. and Salles, M. (eds) 1983: *Social Choice and Welfare*. Amsterdam: North-Holland.

Paul, E.F., Miller, F.D. and Paul, J. (eds) 1985: *Ethics and Economics*. Oxford: Blackwell.

Pazner, E.A. and Schmeidler, D. 1974: A difficulty in the concept of fairness. *Review of Economic Studies*, 41.

Peacock, A.T. and Rowley, C.K. 1972: Welfare economics and the public regulation of natural monopoly. *Journal of Political Economy*, 80.

Peleg, B. 1984: *Game Theoretic Analysis of Voting in Committees*. Cambridge: University Press.

Pen, J. 1971: *Income Distribution: Facts, Theories, Policies*. New York: Praeger.

Perelli-Minetti, C.R. 1977: Nozick on Sen: a misunderstanding. *Theory and Decision*, 8.

Pettit, P. 1980: *Judging Justice: An Introduction to Contemporary Political Philosophy*. London: Routledge.

Phelps, E.S. (eds) 1973: *Economic Justice*. Harmondsworth: Penguin Books.

Phelps, E.S. 1977: Recent developments in welfare economics: justice et équité. In M.D. Intriligator (ed.), *Frontiers of Quantitative Economics*, vol. 3. Amsterdam: North-Holland. Reprinted in his *Studies in Macroeconomic Theory*, vol. 2. New York: Academic Press.

Pigou, A.C. 1952: *The Economics of Welfare*, 4th edition. London: Macmillan.

Pitt, J.C. (ed.) 1981: *Philosophy in Economics*. Dordrecht: Reidel.

Plott, C.R. 1976: Axiomatic social choice theory: an overview and interpretation. *Journal of Political Science*, 20.

Pollak, R.A. 1979: Bergson–Samuelson social welfare functions

112 *References*

and the theory of social choice. *Quarterly Journal of Economics*, 93.

Posner, R.A. 1977: *The Economic Analysis of Law*. Boston: Little, Brown.

Posner, R.A. 1980: A theory of primitive society with special reference to law. *Journal of Law and Economics*, 23.

Putterman, L. 1981: On optimality of collective institutional choice. *Journal of Comparative Economics*, 5.

Putterman, L. 1986: *Peasants, collectives, and choice*. Greenwich, Conn.: JAI Press.

Pyatt, G. 1976: On the interpretation and disaggregation of gini coefficients. *Economic Journal*, 86.

Pyatt, G. 1985: *Measuring Welfare, Poverty and Inequality*, mimeographed. Development Research Department, World Bank, Washington D.C.

Radner, R. 1980: Collusive behaviour in non-cooperative epsilon-equilibria of oligopoplies with long but finite lives. *Journal of Economic Theory*, 22.

Radnitsky, G. and Bernholz, P. (eds) 1985: *Economic Imperialism: The Economic Approach Applied Outside the Traditional Areas of Economics*. New York: Paragon House.

Rae, D. 1981: *Equalities*. Cambridge, Mass.: Harvard University Press.

Ramaswamy, T.N. 1962: *Essentials of Indian Statecraft*. London: Asia Publishing House.

Ramsey, F.P. 1931: *Foundations of Mathematics and Other Logical Essays*. London: Kegan Paul.

Raphael, D.D. 1985: *Adam Smith*. Oxford: University Press.

Raphael, D.D. and Macfie, A.L. 1976: Introduction. In their edited *The Theory of Moral Sentiments*, by Adam Smith. Oxford: Clarendon Press.

Rapoport, A. and Chammah, A.M. 1965: *Prisoner's dilemma: A study in conflict and cooperation*. Ann Arbor: University of Michigan Press.

Rawls, J. 1971: *A Theory of Justice*. Cambridge, Mass.: Harvard University Press.

Rawls, J. 1980: Kantian constructivism in moral theory: the Dewey Lectures 1980. *Journal of Philosophy*, 77.

Rawls, J. 1982: Social unity and primary goods. In Sen and Williams (1982).

Rawls, J. 1985: Justice as fairness: political not metaphysical.

Philosophy and Public Affairs, 14.

Raz, J. 1986: *The Morality of Freedom*. Oxford: Clarendon Press.

Regan, D.H. 1980: *Utilitarianism and Co-operation*. Oxford: Clarendon Press.

Regan, D.H. 1983: Against evaluator relativity: a response to Sen. *Philosophical Public Affairs*, 12.

Richter, M.K. 1971: Rational choice. In Chipman, Richter, Hurwicz and Sonnenschein (1971).

Riley, J. 1986: *Liberal Utilitarianism: Social Choice Theory and J.S. Mill's Philosophy*. Cambridge: University Press in press.

Robbins, L. 1935: *An Essay on the Nature and Significance of Economic Science*, 2nd edition. London: Macmillan.

Robbins, L. 1938: Interpersonal comparisons of utility. *Economic Journal*, 48.

Roberts, K.W.S. 1980a: Interpersonal comparability and social choice theory. *Review of Economic Studies*, 47.

Roberts, K.W.S. 1980b: Price independent welfare prescriptions. *Journal of Public Economics*, 13.

Robinson, J. 1962: *Economic Philosophy*. London: Watts.

Roemer, J. 1982: *A General Theory of Exploitation and Class*. Cambridge, Mass.: Harvard University Press.

Roemer, J. 1985a: Should Marxists be interested in exploitation? *Philosophy and Public Affairs*, 14.

Roemer, J. 1985b: Equality of talent. *Economics and Philosophy*, 1.

Roemer, J. 1986a: Equality of resources implies equality of welfare. *Quarterly Journal of Economics*, forthcoming.

Roemer, J. 1986b: An historical materialist alternative to welfarism. In Elster and Hylland (1986).

Rose-Ackerman, S. 1978: *Corruption: A Study in Political Economy*. New York: Academic Press.

Rosenberg, N. 1984: Adam Smith and the stock of moral capital. Mimeographed, Stanford Univeristy.

Ross, D. ed. 1980: *Aristotle: The Nicomachean Ethics*. Oxford: University Press.

Rothschild, M. and Stiglitz, J. 1973: Some further results in the measurement of inequality. *Journal of Economic Theory*, 6.

Rowley, C.K. and Peacock, A.T. 1975: *Welfare Economics: A Liberal Restatement*. London: Martin Robertson.

Rubinstein, A. 1981: *The Single Profile Analogues to Multiple*

Profile Theorems: Mathematical Logic's Approach. Mimeographed. Murray Hill: Bell Laboratories.

Samuelson, P.A. 1947: *Foundations of Economic Analysis.* Cambridge, Mass.: Harvard University Press.

Samuelson, P.A. 1950: Evaluation of Real National Income. *Oxford Economic Papers*, 2.

Sandel, M.J. 1982: *Liberalism and the Limits of Justice.* Cambridge: University Press.

Sartre. J.-P. 1946: *Existentialisme est un humanisme*, Paris.

Satterthwaite, M.A. 1975: Strategy-proofness and Arrow's conditions: existence and correspondence theorems for voting procedures and social welfare functions. *Journal of Economic Theory*, 10.

Scanlon, T.M. 1975: Preference and urgency. *Journal of Philosophy*, 72.

Scanlon, T.M. 1982: Contractualism and utilitarianism. In Sen and Williams (1982).

Scheffler, S. 1982: *The Rejection of Consequentialism.* Oxford: Clarendon Press.

Schelling, T.C. 1978: *Micromotives and Macrobehavior.* New York: Norton.

Schelling. T.C. 1980: The intimate contest for self-command. *Public Interest*, 60.

Schelling, T.C. 1984: Self-command in practice, in policy, and in a theory of rational choice. *American Economic Review*, 74.

Schick, F. 1984: *Having Reasons: An Essay on Rationality and Sociality.* Princeton: University Press.

Schmeidler, D. and Sonnenschein, H. 1978: Two proofs of the Gibbard–Satterthwaite theorem on the possibility of a strategy-proof social choice function. In Gottinger and Leinfellner (1978).

Schmeidler, D and Vind, K. 1972: Fair net trades. *Econometrica*, 40.

Schotter, A. 1981: *The Economic Theory of Social Institutions.* Cambridge: University Press.

Schotter, A. 1985: *Free Market Economics: A Critical Appraisal.* New York: St. Martin's Press.

Schwartz, T. 1970: On the possibility of rational policy evaluation. *Theory and Decision*, 1.

Schwartz, T. 1976: Choice functions, 'Rationality' conditions, and variations of the weak axiom of revealed preference. *Journal of Economic Theory*, 13.

Schwartz, T. 1981: The Universal Instability Theorem. *Public Choice*, 37.

Schwartz, T. 1982: Human welfare: what it is not. In H. Miller and W. Williams (eds), *The Limits of Utilitarianism*. Minneapolis: University of Minnesota Press.

Schwartz, T. 1986: *The Logic of Collective Choice*. New York: Columbia University Press.

Scitovsky, T. 1941: A note on welfare propositions in economics. *Review of Economic Studies*, 9.

Scitovsky, T. 1976: *The Joyless Economy*. New York: Oxford University Press.

Searle, J. 1980: *Prime facie* Obligations. In Z. van Straaten (ed.), *Philosophical Subjects: Essays Presented to P.F. Strawson*. Oxford: Clarendon Press.

Seidl, C. 1975: On liberal values. *Zeitschrift für Nationalökonomie*, 35.

Seidl, C. 1986: *Poverty Measures: A Survey*. Mimeographed, Graz-Kiel.

Sen, A.K. 1961: On optimizing the rate of saving. *Economic Journal*, 71; reprinted in Sen (1984a).

Sen, A.K. 1966: Labour allocation in a cooperative enterprise. *Review of Economic Studies*, 33; reprinted in Sen (1984a).

Sen, A.K. 1967a: Isolation, assurance and the social rate of discount. *Quarterly Journal of Economics*, 81; reprinted in Sen (1984a).

Sen, A.K. 1967b: The nature and classes of prescriptive judgements. *Philosophical Quarterly*, 17.

Sen, A.K. 1970a: *Collective Choice and Social Welfare*. San Francisco: Holden-Day; republished, Amsterdam: North-Holland, 1979.

Sen, A.K. 1970b: Interpersonal aggregation and partial comparability. *Econometrica*, 38; reprinted in Sen (1982a). A correction, *Econometrica*, 40 (1972).

Sen, A.K. 1970c: The impossibility of a Paretian liberal. *Journal of Political Economy*. 72; reprinted in Sen (1982a).

Sen, A.K. 1971: Choice functions and revealed preference. *Review of Economic Studies*, 38; reprinted in Sen (1982a).

Sen, A.K. 1973a: Behaviour and the concept of preference. *Economica*, 40; reprinted in Sen (1982a).

Sen, A.K. 1973b: *On Economic Inequality*. Oxford: Clarendon Press, and New York: Norton.

Sen, A.K. 1973c: On the development of basic income indicators to supplement GNP measures. *Economic Bulletin for Asia and the Far East* (United Nations), 24.

Sen, A.K. 1974: Choice, orderings and morality. In Korner (1974); reprinted in Sen (1982a).

Sen, A.K. 1976a: Poverty: an ordinal approach to measurement. *Econometrica*, 46; reprinted in Sen (1982a).

Sen, A.K. 1976b: Real national income. *Review of Economic Studies*. 43; reprinted in Sen (1982a).

Sen, A.K. 1976c: Liberty, Unanimity and Rights. *Economica*, 43; reprinted in Sen (1982a).

Sen, A.K. 1977a: Social choice theory: a re-examination. *Econometrica*. 45; reprinted in Sen (1982a).

Sen, A.K. 1977b: On weights and measures: informational constraints in social welfare analysis. *Econometrica*, 45; reprinted in Sen (1982a).

Sen, A.K. 1977c: Rational fools: a critique of the behavioural foundations of economic theory. *Philosophy and Public Affairs*, 6; reprinted in Sen (1982a).

Sen, A.K. 1979a: Personal utilities and public judgments: or what's wrong with welfare economics? *Economic Journal*, 89; reprinted in Sen (1982a).

Sen, A.K. 1979b: Utilitarianism and welfarism. *Journal of Philosophy*, 76.

Sen, A.K. 1979c: The welfare basis of real income comparisons. *Journal of Economic Literature*, 17; reprinted in Sen (1984a).

Sen, A.K. 1980: Equality of what? In McMurrin (1980); reprinted in Sen (1982a).

Sen, A.K. 1981a: *Poverty and Famines: An Essay on Entitlement and Deprivation*. Oxford: Clarendon Press.

Sen, A.K. 1981b: A positive concept of negative freedom. In E. Morscher and R. Stranzinger, (eds), *Ethics: Foundations, Problems, and Applications, Proceedings of the 5th International Wittgenstein Symposium*. Vienna: Holder-Pichler-Tempsky.

Sen, A.K. 1982a: *Choice, Welfare and Measurement*. Oxford: Blackwell, and Cambridge, Mass.: MIT Press.

Sen, A.K. 1982b: Rights and agency. *Philosophy and Public Affairs*, 11.

Sen, A.K. 1983a: Liberty and social choice, *Journal of Philosophy*, 80.

Sen, A.K. 1983b: The profit motive. *Lloyds Bank Review*, 147; reprinted in Sen (1984a).

Sen, A.K. 1983c: Evaluator relativity and consequential evaluation, *Philosophy and Public Affairs*, 12.

Sen, A.K. 1983d: Economics and the family. *Asian Development Review*, 1; reprinted in Sen (1984a).

Sen, A.K. 1984a: *Resources, Values and Development*. Oxford: Blackwell, and Cambridge, Mass.: Harvard University Press.

Sen, A.K. 1984b: The living standard. *Oxford Economic Papers*, 6.

Sen, A.K. 1984c: Consistency, text of Presidential Address to the Econometric Society, to be published in Econometrica.

Sen, A.K. 1985a: Well-being, agency and freedom: the Dewey Lectures 1984. *Journal of Philosophy*, 82.

Sen, A.K. 1985b: *Commodities and Capabilities*. Amsterdam: North-Holland.

Sen, A.K. 1985c: Rights as goals, Austin Lecture 1984. In S. Guest and A. Milne, (eds), *Equality and Discrimination: Essays in Freedom and Justice*. Stuttgart: Franz Steiner.

Sen, A.K. 1985d: Goals, commitment and identity. *Journal of Law, Economics and Organization*, 1.

Sen, A.K. 1985e: Rationality and uncertainty. *Theory and Decision*, 18; also in Daboni, Montesano and Lines (1986).

Sen, A.K. 1985f: Women, technology and sexual divisions. *Trade and Development*, 6.

Sen, A.K. 1985g: The moral standing of the market. In Paul, Miller and Paul (1985).

Sen, A.K. 1986a: Food, economics and entitlements. Elmhirst lecture, 1985. *Lloyds Bank Review*, 160.

Sen, A.K. 1986b: Adam Smith's prudence. In S. Lall and F. Stewart (eds), *Theory and Reality in Development*. London: Macmillan.

Sen, A.K. 1986c: Social choice theory. In K.J. Arrow and M. Intriligator, (eds), *Handbook of Mathematical Economics*, vol. III. Amsterdam: North-Holland.

Sen, A.K. 1986d: Prediction and economic theory. *Proceedings of the Royal Society*.

Sen, A.K. 1986e: The standard of living. In S. McMurrin, *Tanner Lectures on Human Values*, vol. VII. Cambridge: University Press.

Sen, A.K. 1986f: Information and invariance in normative

118 References

choice. In W. Heller, D. Starr and R. Starrett (1986).

Sen, A.K. and Williams, B. (eds) 1982: *Utilitarianism and Beyond*. Cambridge: University Press.

Sen, A.K., with Hart, K., Kanbur, R., Muellbauer, J., Williams, B., and (ed) Hawthorn, G. 1987: *The Standard of Living*. Cambridge: University Press.

Shama Sastry, R. 1967: *Kautilya's Arthaśāstra, Mysore: Mysore Printing and Publishing House*.

Sheshinski, E. 1972: *Relation between social welfare function and the Gini index of inequality. Journal of Economic Theory*, 4.

Shorrocks, A.F. 1980: The class of additively decomposable inequality measures. *Econometrica*, 48.

Shorrocks, A.F. 1983: Ranking income distributions. *Economica*, 50.

Shorrocks, A.F. 1984: Inequality decomposition by population subgroups. *Econometrica*, 52.

Shorrocks, A.F. and Foster, J.E. 1985: *Transfer Sensitive Inequality Measures*. Department of Economics, University of Essex.

Sidgwick, H. 1874: *The Method of Ethics*. London: Macmillan.

Sil, N.P. 1985: Kautilya's Arthaśāstra. Calcutta: Academic Publishers.

Simon, H.A. 1957: *Models of Man*. New York: Wiley.

Simon, H.A. 1979: *Models of Thought*. New Haven: Yale University Press.

Skinner, A.S. and Wilson, T. (eds) 1975: *Essays on Adam Smith*. Oxford: Clarendon Press.

Slote, M. 1983: *Goods and Virtues*. Oxford: Clarendon Press.

Slote, M. 1985: *Common-sense Morality and Consequentialism*. London: Routledge.

Smale S. 1980: The prisoner's dilemma and dynamic systems associated to non-cooperative games. *Econometrica*, 48.

Smart, J.J.C. and Williams, B.A.O. 1973: *Utilitarianism: For and Against*. Cambridge: University Press.

Smith, A. 1776: *An Inquiry into the Nature and Causes of the Wealth of Nations*. Reprinted R.H. Campbell and A.S. Skinner (eds). Oxford: Clarendon Press.

Smith, A. 1790: *The Theory of Moral Sentiments*, revised edition. Reprinted, D.D. Raphael and A.L. Macfie (eds). Oxford: Clarendon Press, 1975.

Solow, R.M. 1980: On theories of unemployment. *American Economic Review*, 70.

Srinivasan, T.N. 1981: Malnutrition: some measurement and policy issues. *Journal of Development Economics*, 8.

Srinivasan, T.N. and Bardhan, P. (eds) 1986: *Rural Poverty in South Asia*, to be published by Columbia University Press.

Starr, R.M. 1973: Optimum production and allocation under uncertainty. *Quarterly Journal of Economics*, 87.

Steedman, I. and Krause, U. 1986: Goethe's Faust, Arrow's possibility theorem and the individual decision taker. In J. Elster (ed.), *The Multiple Self*. Cambridge: University Press.

Steiner H. 1981: Liberty and equality. *Political Studies*, 29.

Steiner, H. 1983: Reason and intuition in ethics. *Ratio*, 25.

Steiner, H. 1986: *Putting rights in their place: an appraisal of Amartya Sen's work on rights*. Mimeographed, University of Manchester.

Stevens, D. and Foster, J. 1978: The possibility of democratic pluralism, *Economica*, 45.

Stewart, F. 1985: *Planning to Meet Basic Needs*. London: Macmillan.

Stigler, G.J. 1975: Smith's travel on the ship of the state. In Skinner and Wilson (1975).

Stigler, G.J. 1981: Economics or ethics? In S. McMurrin (ed.), *Tanner Lectures on Human Values*, vol. II, Cambridge: University Press.

Stigum, B.P. and Wenstop, F. (eds) 1983: *Foundations of Utility and Risk Theory with Applications*. Dordrecht: Reidel.

Strasnick, S. 1976: Social choice theory and the derivation of Rawls' difference principle. *Journal of Philosophy*, 73.

Streeten, P. 1981a: *Development Perspectives*. London: Macmillan.

Streeten, P. 1981b: With S.J. Burki, Mahbub ul Haq, N. Hicks and F. Stewart, *First Things First: Meeting Basic Needs in Developing Countries*. New York: Oxford University Press.

Streeten, P. and Burki, S. 1978: Basic needs: some issues. *World Development*, 6.

Sugden, R. 1981: *The Political Economy of Public Choice*. Oxford: Martin Robertson.

Sugden, R. 1985: Liberty, preference and choice. *Economics and Philosophy*, 1.

Suppes, P. 1966: Some formal models of grading principles. *Synthese*, 6; reprinted in Suppes (1969).

Suppes, P. 1969: *Studies in the Methodology and Foundations of Science*. Dordrecht: Reidel.

Suzumura, K. 1976: Rational choice and revealed preference. *Review of Economic Studies*, 43.

Suzumura, K. 1978: On the Consistency of Libertarian Claims, *Review of Economic Studies*, 45: A correction, 46.

Suzumura, K. 1980: Liberal paradox and the voluntary exchange of rights-exercising. *Journal of Economic Theory*, 22.

Suzumura, K. 1983: *Rational Choice, Collective Decisions, and Social Welfare*. Cambridge: University Press.

Svensson. L.-G. 1977: Social justice and fair distributions, *Lund Economic Studies*, 15.

Svensson, L.-G. 1980: Equity among generations. *Econometrica*, 48.

Svensson, L.-G. 1985: A contractarian approach to social optimum. Mimeographed, University of Lund.

Takayama, N. 1979: Poverty, income inequality and their measures: Professor Sen's axiomatic approach reconsidered. *Econometrica*, 47.

Taylor, C. 1982: The diversity of goods. In Sen and Williams (1982).

Taylor, L. 1977: Research directions in income distribution, nutrition and the economics of food. *Food Research Institute Studies*, 15.

Taylor, M. 1976: *Anarchy and Cooperation*. New York: Wiley.

Temkin, L. 1986: Inequality, *Philosophy and Public Affairs*, 15.

Theil, H. 1967: *Economics and Information Theory*. Amsterdam: North-Holland.

Thon, D. 1979: On measuring poverty. *Review of Income and Wealth*, 25.

Tinbergen, J. 1970: A Positive and Normative Theory of Income Distribution. *Review of Income and Wealth*, 16.

Ullman-Margalitt, E. 1977: *The Emergence of Norms*. Oxford: Clarendon Press.

Usher, D. 1981: *The Economic Prerequisite to Democracy*. Oxford: Blackwell.

Van der Veen, R.J. 1981: Meta-rankings and collective optimality. *Social Science Information*, 20.

Van Praag, B.M.S. 1968: *Individual Welfare Functions and Consumer Behaviour*. Amsterdam: North-Holland.

Van Praag, B.M.S. 1977: The welfare function of income in Belgium: an empirical investigation, *European Economic Review*, 2.

Van Praag, B.M.S. 1978: The perception of welfare inequality. *European Economic Review*, 2.

Van Praag, B.M.S. and Kapteyn, A. 1973: Further evidence on the individual welfare function of income: an empirical investigation in the Netherlands, *European Economic Review*, 4.

Varian, H. 1974: Equity, envy and efficiency, *Journal of Economic Theory*, 9.

Varian, H. 1975: Distributive justice, welfare economics and the theory of fairness, *Philosophy and Public Affairs*, 4.

Vickrey, W. 1945: Measuring marginal utility by reactions to risk. *Econometrica*, 13.

Waldron, J. (ed) 1984: *Theories of Rights*. Oxford: University Press.

Walzer, M. 1973: Political action: the problem of dirty hands. *Philosophy and Public Affairs*, 2.

Walzer, M. 1983: *Spheres of Justice*. Oxford: Blackwell.

Ward, B. 1972: *What's Wrong with Economics?* London: Macmillan.

Watkins, J. 1974: Comment: self-interest and morality. In Korner (1974).

Watkins, J. 1985: Second thoughts on self-interest and morality. In Campbell and Sowden (1985).

Weale, A. 1978: *Equality and Social Policy*. London: Routledge & Kegan Paul.

Weale, A. 1980: The impossibility of liberal egalitarianism. *Analysis*, 40.

Webster, M. 1986: Liberals and information. *Theory and Decisions*, 20.

Weymark, J. 1978: 'Unselfishness' and Prisoner's Dilemma. *Philosophical Studies*, 34.

Weymark, J. 1983: Arrow's theorem with social quasi-orderings. *Public Choice*, 42.

Wiggins, D. 1985: Claims of need. In Honderich (1985).

Williams, B.A.O. 1973a: A critique of utilitarianism. In Smart and Williams (1973).

Williams, B.A.O. 1973b: *Problems of the Self*. Cambridge: University Press.

Williams, B.A.O. 1981: *Moral Luck*. Cambridge: University Press.

Williams, B.A.O. 1985: *Ethics and the Limits of Philosophy*.

London: Fontana; and Cambridge, Mass.: Harvard University Press.

Wilson, E.O. 1978: *On Human Nature*. Cambridge, Mass.: Harvard University Press.

Wilson, E.O. 1980: Comparative Social Theory. In McMurrin (1980).

Wilson, R.B. 1975: On the theory of aggregation. *Journal of Economics*, 10.

Winch, D. 1978: *Adam Smith's Politics*. Cambridge: University Press.

Winston, G.C. 1980: Addiction and back-sliding: a theory of compulsive consumption. *Journal of Economic Behaviour and Organisation*, 1.

Winter, S.G. 1969: A simple remark on the second optimality theorem of welfare economics. *Journal of Economic Theory*, 1.

Wittman, D. 1984: The geometry of justice: three existence and uniqueness theorems. *Theory and Decision*, 165.

Wong, S. 1978: *Foundations of Paul Samuelson's Revealed Preference Theory*. London: Routledge & Kegan Paul.

Woo, H.K.H. 1986: *What's Wrong with Formalization in Economics?* Newark, Cal.: Victoria Press.

Wriglesworth, J. 1982: The possibility of democratic pluralism: a comment, *Economica*, 49.

Wriglesworth, J. 1985: *Libertarian Conflicts in Social Choice*. Cambridge: University Press.

Yaari, M.E. and Bar-Hilell, M. 1984: On dividing justly. *Social Choice and Welfare*, 1.

Young, H.P. 1986: *Fair Allocation*, to be published by the American Mathematical Society.

Author Index

Subject Index